A CELEBRATION
OF POETS

SOUTH
GRADES K-3
FALL 2009

creativeCOMMUNICATION
A CELEBRATION OF TODAY'S WRITERS

A CELEBRATION OF POETS
SOUTH
GRADES K-3
FALL 2009

AN ANTHOLOGY COMPILED BY CREATIVE COMMUNICATION, INC.

Published by:

creativeCOMMUNICATION
A CELEBRATION OF TODAY'S WRITERS

1488 NORTH 200 WEST • LOGAN, UTAH 84341
TEL. 435-713-4411 • WWW.POETICPOWER.COM

ISBN: 978-1-60050-322-1

FOREWORD

In today's world there are many things that compete for our attention. From the far reaching influence of the media, to the voices we hear from those around us, it is often difficult to decide where to commit our energies and focus. The poets in this book listened to an inner voice; a voice that can be the loudest of the many voices in our world, but to pay attention to this voice takes self-control. The effect of these words may not be far reaching, but to even make a small difference in the world is a positive thing.

Each year I receive hundreds of letters, calls, and emails from parents, teachers, and students who share stories of success; stories, where being a published writer provided the catalyst to a different attitude toward school, education and life. We are pleased to provide you with this book and hope that what these writers have shared makes a small but meaningful difference in your world.

Thomas Worthen, Ph.D.
Editor
Creative Communication

WRITING CONTESTS!

Enter our next POETRY contest!
Enter our next ESSAY contest!

Why should I enter?

Win prizes and get published! Each year thousands of dollars in prizes are awarded throughout North America. The top writers in each division receive a monetary award and a free book that includes their published poem or essay. Entries of merit are also selected to be published in our anthology.

Who may enter?

There are four divisions in the poetry contest. The poetry divisions are grades K-3, 4-6, 7-9, and 10-12. There are three divisions in the essay contest. The essay divisions are grades 3-6, 7-9, and 10-12.

What is needed to enter the contest?

To enter the poetry contest send in one original poem, 21 lines or less. To enter the essay contest send in one original non-fiction essay, 250 words or less, on any topic. Each entry must include the student's name, grade, address, city, state, and zip code, and the student's school name and school address. Students who include their teacher's name may help their teacher qualify for a free copy of the anthology. Contest changes and updates are listed at www.poeticpower.com.

How do I enter?

Enter a poem online at:
www.poeticpower.com
or
Mail your poem to:
   Poetry Contest
   1488 North 200 West
   Logan, UT 84341

Enter an essay online at:
www.studentessaycontest.com
or
Mail your essay to:
   Essay Contest
   1488 North 200 West
   Logan, UT 84341

When is the deadline?

Poetry contest deadlines are August 18th, December 2nd, and April 5th. Essay contest deadlines are July 15th, October 19th, and February 17th. Students can enter one poem and one essay for each spring, summer, and fall contest deadline.

Are there benefits for my school?

Yes. We award $15,000 each year in grants to help with Language Arts programs. Schools qualify to apply for a grant by having 15 or more accepted entries.

Are there benefits for my teacher?

Yes. Teachers with five or more students published receive a free anthology that includes their students' writing.

For more information please go to our website at
www.poeticpower.com,
email us at editor@poeticpower.com or call 435-713-4411.

TABLE OF CONTENTS

STATES INCLUDED IN THIS EDITION:

Alabama
Arkansas
Florida
Georgia
Kentucky
Louisiana
Mississippi
Missouri
North Carolina
Oklahoma
South Carolina
Tennessee
West Virginia

Fall 2009 Poetic Achievement Honor Schools

* Teachers who had fifteen or more poets accepted to be published

The following schools are recognized as receiving a "Poetic Achievement Award." This award is given to schools who have a large number of entries of which over fifty percent are accepted for publication. With hundreds of schools entering our contest, only a small percent of these schools are honored with this award. The purpose of this award is to recognize schools with excellent Language Arts programs. This award qualifies these schools to receive a complimentary copy of this anthology. In addition, these schools are eligible to apply for a Creative Communication Language Arts Grant. Grants of two hundred and fifty dollars each are awarded to further develop writing in our schools.

A H Watwood Elementary School
Childersburg, AL
  Denise Ivey*

Alpena Elementary School
Alpena, AR
  Sherry Choate
  Jeanie Daniels
  Holly Kelley
  Dawn Keys*
  Stella Maberry
  Kiersten Wray

Bramlett Elementary School
Auburn, GA
  Mary Kay Farr*

Briarwood Christian School
Birmingham, AL
  Martha Bickford
  Joie Black
  Amy Bryant*
  Jenny Burdick
  Jill Byrd*
  Pam Chastain*
  Kari Cuenin*
  Tammy Cuneo*
  Kristin Fincher
  Jennie Gillon
  Debbie Griffin*
  Lisha Hutchinson*
  Susan Johnson*
  Katie Kirkpatrick*
  Danielle Lieb*

Briarwood Christian School (cont.)
Birmingham, AL
Alison McKeen*
Emily McNutt
Lauren Meadows*
Marion Petty
Joy Phillips
Mary Ann Pickell
Paige Robinson
Cynthia Rushing
Charlotte Smith
Staci Wagner
Cheryl Young

Buckner Elementary School
Buckner, KY
Heather Cook*
Emily Doyle*
Holly Dunigan*
Nicole Walker

Camden Station Elementary School
Crestwood, KY
Megan Adams*
Shawna Allen*
Mona Cahela*
Rene Larkin*
Courtney Lowe*

Caneview Elementary School
New Iberia, LA
Susan Andrus
Rebecca Champagne
Mandy Glaubrecht
Brenda Istre
Nancy Justice
Angie Migues
Laney Rodrigue
Laura Segura

Carver Elementary School
Henderson, NC
Mrs. Abbott
Savi Sandhu

Central Park Elementary School
Plantation, FL
Mary Buscemi
Kristen Marsolek*
Mark Siegel*

Cool Spring Elementary School
Cleveland, NC
Tonya Cassidy*
Stephanie Flammang
Pam Long
Sandra Milholland*
Monica Williams

Doyle Elementary School
Livingston, LA
Tiffany S. Jones*

Evangel Christian Academy
Montgomery, AL
Dena Bittle*
Laura Ryals
Mrs. Spencer

Evangelical Christian School
Germantown, TN
Lindy Murley
Jenny Shorten*

Guardian Angels Catholic School
Clearwater, FL
Debbie Mahle
Patricia Powers

Hunter GT Magnet Elementary School
Raleigh, NC
Lisa Kaszycki
Angie Parham*

Kerr Elementary School
Tulsa, OK
Carolyn Fleming*

Landmark Christian School
Peachtree City, GA
Kim Hermecz
Kimberly Stevens

Lee A Tolbert Community Academy
Kansas City, MO
Angela Boley
Piper Crawford
Zanova Gasaway
Valerie Guy
Nicole McCleish
Rayma Moburg
Lydia Nash
Kate Rowlett
Debbie Sager
Cindy Salomone
Debbie Wunsch
Janice Yocum*

Macon-East Montgomery Academy
Cecil, AL
Mrs. Bocchino
Renee Burch*
Gwen Walters

Mineral Wells Elementary School
Mineral Wells, WV
Marsha Brady*
Bill Fletcher
Ernest Haynes
Darcella Maul
Brenda McKnight*
Randy Modesitt
Greg Rymer

New York Elementary School
Hamilton, MO
Dee Adkison
Candy Hughes

Northeast Baptist School
West Monroe, LA
Lisa Navarro
Diane Tidwell

Oakland Primary School
Sumter, SC
Alberta Barrett-Johnson*
Joyce Boyd
Bridgett Bradley
Aleshia Conyers
Irene Davis
Mary Eason
Lakesha Grant
Patricia Green
Antionette Hampton
Margaret Lybrand*
Taran McCray
Sheri Palmo
Lakeisha Wells
Alice Wright

Orlando Junior Academy
Orlando, FL
Sharon Coldren*

Ponte Vedra Palm Valley
Elementary School
Ponte Vedra Beach, FL
Rita Andreu*

Rivelon Elementary School
Orangeburg, SC
Denise J.
Brown-Johnson*
Darlene Daniels*
Patricia Hampton
Cedrick Sweeper
Tonya Yarbrough

Riverhill School
Florence, AL
Morgan Ary
Mrs. McAlpin
Mrs. Newell

Robert E Lee Expressive Arts
Elementary School
Columbia, MO
Nancy Bond
Diane Gilbert
Linda Poehlmann*

The Parke House Academy
Winter Park, FL
Marisa Lyendecker
Kimberly
Murphy-Thompson

Virginia A Boone Highland
Oaks Elementary School
North Miami Beach, FL
Terri Cohen*
Phillis Diskin
Marilyn Herman
Stephanie Sheir*

Wellington School
Saint Petersburg, FL
Marilynn Daniels
Wendy Genzel
Meredith Wakefield

Westlake Christian School
Palm Harbor, FL
Mary Barbaccia*
Kimberly Fleming*

Language Arts Grant Recipients 2009-2010

After receiving a "Poetic Achievement Award" schools are encouraged to apply for a Creative Communication Language Arts Grant. The following is a list of schools who received a two hundred and fifty dollar grant for the 2009-2010 school year.

Arrowhead Union High School, Hartland, WI
Blessed Sacrament School, Seminole, FL
Booneville Jr High School, Booneville, AR
Buckhannon-Upshur Middle School, Buckhannon, WV
Campbell High School, Ewa Beach, HI
Chickahominy Middle School, Mechanicsville, VA
Clarkston Jr High School, Clarkston, MI
Covenant Life School, Gaithersburg, MD
CW Rice Middle School, Northumberland, PA
Eason Elementary School, Waukee, IA
East Elementary School, Kodiak, AK
Florence M Gaudineer Middle School, Springfield, NJ
Foxborough Regional Charter School, Foxborough, MA
Gideon High School, Gideon, MO
Holy Child Academy, Drexel Hill, PA
Home Choice Academy, Vancouver, WA
Jeff Davis Elementary School, Biloxi, MS
Lower Alloways Creek Elementary School, Salem, NJ
Maple Wood Elementary School, Somersworth, NH
Mary Walter Elementary School, Bealeton, VA
Mater Dei High School, Evansville, IN
Mercy High School, Farmington Hills, MI
Monroeville Elementary School, Monroeville, OH

Language Arts Grant Winners cont.

Nautilus Middle School, Miami Beach, FL
Our Lady Star of the Sea School, Grosse Pointe Woods, MI
Overton High School, Memphis, TN
Pond Road Middle School, Robbinsville, NJ
Providence Hall Charter School, Herriman, UT
Reuben Johnson Elementary School, McKinney, TX
Rivelon Elementary School, Orangeburg, SC
Rose Hill Elementary School, Omaha, NE
Runnels School, Baton Rouge, LA
Santa Fe Springs Christian School, Santa Fe Springs, CA
Serra Catholic High School, Mckeesport, PA
Shadowlawn Elementary School, Green Cove Springs, FL
Spectrum Elementary School, Gilbert, AZ
St Edmund Parish School, Oak Park, IL
St Joseph Institute for the Deaf, Chesterfield, MO
St Joseph Regional Jr High School, Manchester, NH
St Mary of Czestochowa School, Middletown, CT
St Monica Elementary School, Garfield Heights, OH
St Vincent De Paul Elementary School, Cape Girardeau, MO
Stevensville Middle School, Stevensville, MD
Tashua School, Trumbull, CT
The New York Institute for Special Education, Bronx, NY
The Selwyn School, Denton, TX
Tonganoxie Middle School, Tonganoxie, KS
Westside Academy, Prince George, BC
Willa Cather Elementary School, Omaha, NE
Willow Hill Elementary School, Traverse City, MI

Grades K-1-2-3
Top Ten Winners

List of Top Ten Winners for Grades K-3; listed alphabetically

Aydin Cruz, Grade 3
Clayville School, Clayville, RI

Aditya Desai, Grade 2
Beaver Creek Elementary School, Johnston, IA

Will Dougherty, Kindergarten
Evangelical Christian School, Germantown, TN

Stephanie Edds, Grade 3
Buckner Elementary School, Buckner, KY

Lucas Fumiatti, Grade 3
Jeffrey Elementary School, Madison, CT

Jessica Leitenberger, Grade 3
Dousman Elementary School, Dousman, WI

Emma Merlini, Grade 2
Ponte Vedra Palm Valley Elementary School, Ponte Vedra Beach, FL

Hannah Perkins, Grade 3
Mary Walter Elementary School, Bealeton, VA

Bailey Tuttle, Grade 3
Silver Creek Elementary School, Thornton, CO

Maxwell VanLandschoot, Grade 3
Peabody Elementary School, Centennial, CO

All Top Ten Poems can be read at www.poeticpower.com

Note: The Top Ten poems were finalized through an online voting system. Creative Communication's judges first picked out the top poems. These poems were then posted online. The final step involved thousands of students and teachers who registered as the online judges and voted for the Top Ten poems. We hope you enjoy these selections.

Christmas Day
I taste
The warm gingerbread cookies right out of the oven
The minty little candy canes tall or short
The chocolate all wrapped nice
I see
My whole family all around me
All my gifts around me big and small
Santa's cookies by a glass of milk

I smell
A lot of my mom's cooking
Minty candles all in the kitchen
A big Christmas tree
I hear
My family talking to each other
Santa's sleigh bells ringing while everyone is going to bed

I feel
Good about all my family together
Warm under my covers and so tired as I go to sleep
I know
My family loves me and they love to spend time with me.
We love Jesus and each other.

Abigail McGee, Grade 3
Riverhill School, AL

Sled Ride
When I look outside
my face begins to glow
because we just got
a new blanket of snow.

I put on my boots
to walk to the shed
I open the door
and look for my sled.

Down the hill I go
with my dad by my side
to pull me back up
and go for another ride.

Avery Wood, Grade 3
Washington Lands Elementary School, WV

My Rainbow

My rainbow is red and blue
Bright and true.
Purple and pink
Pretty don't you think?
Yellow and green
Just waiting to be seen.
The colors of the rainbow make me feel good
So when you look up
My rainbow has a smile for you.

Anne Thomas, Grade 3
Tri-County Christian School, MO

The Falling

The rain is falling.
The birds are calling.
The sun is shining.
It is blinding.
I don't know why it is blinding.
I guess the sun is shining brightly.
The wind is blowing nicely through my icy.
I hear the ice cream truck coming.
I love the taste of icy icy ice cream.

Abigail Dean, Grade 3
Alpena Elementary School, AR

Blue

Blue is like the sky on a bright day.
Blue is a sad face.
Blue is like a beautiful violet flower.
Blue is like the berries in grandma's blueberry cobbler.
Blue is the color of my fuzzy pajamas.
Blue is the beautiful ocean in Hawaii.

Briauna Thompson, Grade 3
Evangel Christian Academy, AL

The Bear Who Didn't Like to Share

Once there was a bear who didn't like to share.
He gathered all the honey in the land.
Even the dirty honey in the sand.
He stole honey from the big bad bear's cave,
He followed the road that was paved.

Andrea Bautista, Grade 3
Northridge Christian School, OK

Bugs Bugs Bugs

bugs bugs
beetles are bugs
beetles fly
beetles shine in the daylight sun

bugs bugs
ticks crawl
ticks are amazing
ticks are black

bugs bugs
worms make art
worms can be straight
worms squiggle

bugs bugs
crickets jump
crickets crawl
crickets crunch
bugs bugs

Corton Olver, Grade 1
Olver Home School, GA

Green

The tree —
Green, soft, rough, smooth, unscented

The tree —
At Christmas,
As beautiful as it can be

So colorful
Nice
Maybe even to mice

Maybe old, maybe new
Maybe rough, maybe smooth
Sharp and cold on Christmas Day too

Not really blue
But maybe as nice as you!

Riley Wilson, Grade 3
Landmark Christian School, GA

Garden

Walk in the garden of roses
A garden of daisies and tulips.
Beautiful music playing in your ears.
Trickling of the big blue pond
A white trellis, green vines upon it.
The buttery yellow sun goes down
You go home.
Hidden owls come out,
Crickets play their songs.
You lay on your bed
Waiting,
Just waiting
For the sun to come out
And smile at you the very next day!

Emily Pickens, Grade 3
Camden Station Elementary School, KY

The Dart

I am a dart.
I am always on target.
When I hit the bull's eye,
I score big points.

When I miss,
I fall and fall,
And hit the ground
With a thud.

I have a sharp point,
So some kids don't like me,
But some people do,
And I like them, too.

Jack Washburn, Grade 3
Sabal Point Elementary School, FL

My Family

My mom is cool.
My dad is a good cook.
My brother plays with his puppy.
I play with my doll every day.
I love my family very much.

Ariannah Johnson, Grade 1
Oakland Primary School, SC

Fall

The squeaking of screen doors
Color and sounds galore.

The rustling of the leaves,
The buzzing of the bees

The crickets are chirping
The flowers smell sweet

The bushes are prickly
Brown, red, and pink

The birds they are beautiful
Their blue, yellow, and orange

The bugs are small
Green, bumpy, and smooth

Winter is here
Is it over so soon?

Zoe Gilliam, Grade 3
Westminster Christian Academy, GA

Puppy

Wet moist tongue
Making me feel better
When I am sad

Smooth black fur
Shining in the sun
Like diamonds
Running in the yard

Sweet brown eyes
Like a candy bar
In a candy store
I would pay $500
To see her every day

Long fast legs
When she runs
It's funny
Like a bull after a cowboy
Lilly my puppy

Dillon Bickley, Grade 3
Camden Station Elementary School, KY

My Family

My family lives in Clarksville.
There are 4 of us.
We share toys and my games.
We usually don't agree.
And still we are a family.

Our hair is brown.
Are eyes are brown.
Our skin is white, too.
We're all that we can be;
That's why I love my family.

We laugh and play,
We work and laugh,
We hug each other every day.
The world's a wonderful place to be;
Because, we are a family.

Mark Rye, Grade 1
Byrns L Darden Elementary School, TN

My Family

My family lives in Clarksville.
There are 5 of us.
We share toys.
We do agree.
And still we are a family.

Our hair is brown.
Our eyes are brown.
Our skin is brown, too.
We're all that we can be;
That's why I love my family.

We laugh and talk,
We work and we play,
We kiss each other every day.
The world's a good place to be;
Because, we are a family.

Alicia Hicks, Grade 1
Byrns L Darden Elementary School, TN

Camping with My Dad
The sweet smell of the forest
Different types of trees surrounding me
As the kids yelling and screaming
Then the bell the very loud bell
Screaming in my ears time for lunch
All of the kids rushing toward the cafeteria
We get to the cafeteria
The sweet smell of Sunkist wanting to be drank
We find a seat
I take a sip of the Sunkist
Tingles my mouth as it goes down my throat
Then they call our pack the bears
We get up and went where we get food
Hot dogs, applesauce, macaroni and cheese, chips
They taste so very good
Then we finish our wonderful lunch
Then it happens it started to rain
We watch a movie
To keep our mind off the rain
I love the sweet smells of camping
I love being with Dad

Sean Howard, Grade 3
Buckner Elementary School, KY

If I Were Eighteen
If I were eighteen
I would find me a job
and buy a house of my own.
I would buy myself a cell phone,
a TV for my car and graduate from college.
I would have my little sister over
and remember when she was two
and climbed over the couch like a monkey.
I would take my brother for a car ride
and remember when he was one year old
and so handsome for a little guy.
My mom and I would go to dinner
and remember when she was twenty-six
and made sure we were
as beautiful as her.

Ay'riana Jones, Grade 3
Lee A Tolbert Community Academy, MO

My Dirt Bike

I like to ride my dirt bike very fast.
With my helmet on and my chest plate too,
I jump my ramp and do doughnuts too.
I like to ride every day.
So when I get out of school,
Please, don't rain.

Taijuan Richardson, Grade 1
Oakland Primary School, SC

Puppies

Puppies are fun and like to run.
Puppies chase tails and grow long nails.
Puppies chase cats but don't like rats.
Puppies dig holes but never dig far enough to reach a mole.
Puppies play with balls but aren't very tall.
I like puppies don't you?

Hannah Larsen, Grade 2
Evangelical Christian School, TN

Purple Blanket

My favorite color is purple.
My Bratz blanket is purple.
It is soft and makes me feel safe.
I sleep with it all the time.
It's the best when it comes out of the dryer.
I love it when it's warm and smells clean.

Ashleigh Deibel, Grade 1
Oakland Primary School, SC

Friends

Olivia and I are the best of friends,
When we are together the fun never ends!
We love to sing and dance,
We wish we could go to France!

Jenna Katzman, Grade 3
Virginia A Boone Highland Oaks Elementary School, FL

Grass

Grass is on the ground.
It is surrounded by rocks.
Grass is really cool.

Xyon Hadley, Grade 2
Virginia A Boone Highland Oaks Elementary School, FL

Jalen
Jalen
lovable, caring
wild, praying, entertaining
being a Christian
JayBo, Zack
Jalen Hunter, Grade 3
Briarwood Christian School, AL

Grant
Grant
encouraging, gentle
throwing, kicking, typing
always have trusting friends
Grantster
Grant Dowlen, Grade 3
Briarwood Christian School, AL

Callie
Callie
smart, quiet
piano, tennis, gymnastics
truthful to my friends
calculator
Callie Ware, Grade 3
Briarwood Christian School, AL

Joseph's Story Telling
Joseph
goofy, interesting
football, wrestling, 4-wheeling
playing with his friends
Jo Jo
Trinity M. Tew, Grade 3
Briarwood Christian School, AL

Mackenzie
Mackenzie
funny, kind
dancer, cheerleader, singer
pray every single day
Kenzie
Mackenzie King, Grade 3
Briarwood Christian School, AL

Blake
Blake
kind, honest
basketball, football, running
always trust in God
Blake
Blake Hollingsworth, Grade 3
Briarwood Christian School, AL

Caroline
Caroline
kind, awesome
loving, incredible, sweet
I care for others
Carolina
Caroline Grantham, Grade 3
Briarwood Christian School, AL

Amelia
Amelia
thoughtful, patient
piano, violin, singing
friendship will last forever
Half Pint
Amelia Ray, Grade 3
Briarwood Christian School, AL

Zane
Zane
Creative, colorful
Helping, praying, reading
Friends together there forever
Zanyboo
Zane Scaini, Grade 3
Briarwood Christian School, AL

Dreamer
Delaney
Funny, special
Singing, skateboarding, playing
A playful, loyal friend
Laneybug
Delaney Tinsley, Grade 3
Briarwood Christian School, AL

The Awesome Fire Truck
It's big and red.
It has a hose, ladder and tools.
It has a big tank with water
to put out the fire.
It's fast and makes a loud noise
when it's coming.
Terrell Mason, Grade 1
Oakland Primary School, SC

Christ
C hristian-like.
H ow much He loves us!
R edeemer.
I ntelligent.
S aved us from our sins.
T old about His Father.
Jake Wyrosdick, Grade 2
Macon-East Montgomery Academy, AL

Christmas Tree
There was a tree
It was pretty as pretty can be.
On top of the tree was a star
You could see it from very far.
The tree was all bright.
It shined through the night.
John Dawson Sasser, Grade 2
Macon-East Montgomery Academy, AL

The Key
I am a key,
A gold and shiny key.
I am your key.
I'm the one and only key
That will unlock your door
To succeed in everything.
Ricky Parsons, Grade 3
Sabal Point Elementary School, FL

Taylor
Lover of math.
Who feels happy.
Who needs food and water.
Who gives pictures.
Who fears big spiders.
Who lives to see my family.
Taylor Ballard, Grade 1
Doyle Elementary School, LA

Fall Leaves
Purple, yellow, brown
When the wind blows,
They all fall to the ground.
Yellow, purple, brown fall.
Our Lord God
Made them all.
Madison Graf, Grade 2
Eagle's View Academy, FL

Horses
H ot sun beating down on her
O ne little angel
R unning faster and faster
S omething so beautiful
E asy to love
S omeone is riding her away
Aria Spencer, Grade 2
Branson Elementary School, MO

My Pet Class Lizard
We have a pet class lizard.
She is awake right now.
She eats flakes and drinks water.
She is the coolest lizard I have ever seen.
Her name is Lizzy.
I love our pet class lizard.
Dylan Prevette, Grade 2
Cool Spring Elementary School, NC

All About People

Mivi
funny, friendly
swimming, soccer, singing
nice to other people
Miv-Biv
Alexandria Smith, Grade 3
Briarwood Christian School, AL

All About Drew

Drew
nice, jokes
baseball, football, basketball
kind to other people
Drew
Ellie Sherrod, Grade 3
Briarwood Christian School, AL

Fish

F lop
I cky
S wim
H op
Jonathan Level, Grade 3
Pottsville Elementary School, AR

Luke

L uke loves football.
U ses a football every day.
K ick off season is the best.
E specially the Super Bowl.
Luke Dezember, Grade 3
Sacred Heart Elementary School, TN

Drip

A rain drop drips and drips
Rather like drops
It drips and drops upon the ground
And then plop makes a sound.
Emily Lloyd, Grade 3
Columbia Catholic School, MO

Little Catzilla

Little Catzilla,
On his feet all the time,
Jumps on my bed,
Now he's chasing a mouse,
He always gets out of the house.
He tears up the couch
And gets in a little hole.
His tiny cat eyes glow in the dark,
But when midnight comes,
Catzilla falls sound asleep.
Lucas Keller, Grade 2
Cool Spring Elementary School, NC

Dirt Bike

Waking up one morning to
the roaring of the dirt bike
standing in the cold blistering wind
waiting and waiting my turn finally
my turn zooming very fast
my five laps.
Were over fast watching
him
speed
down our path.
Paeton Robinette, Grade 3
Buckner Elementary School, KY

I Am Thankful

I am thankful for my family.
They give me hugs and kisses.
I am grateful for the hand-me-downs
I get from my cousins,
and I appreciate my teacher
because she makes me smart.
I am grateful for my classmates,
that help me with my work,
and for my sisters that get on my nerves,
but give me the stuff that they don't want.
Lauren Anderson, Grade 2
Lee A Tolbert Community Academy, MO

I Want a World Where...

I want a world where...
The leaves dance like a marching band.
I can hear grasshoppers talking to me.
I can hear the moon calling my name.
Summer is always my friend.
The night is like the day.
My mom is as beautiful as a cloud.
I'm a beast in basketball.
Zamoni and Ariyanna are two peas in a pod.
I want a world...

Zamoni Oliver, Grade 3
Rivelon Elementary School, SC

My Kangaroo

She didn't jump over anything —
A platypus
A dingo
A frilled lizard
A wombat with a naked nose
A koala hanging by its toes
A kookaburra
A lorikeet
A sulphur-crested cockatoo —
She jumped over things because she wanted to.

Kaylin McAlexander, Grade 1
Blessed Sacrament School, FL

My Birthday Bunny

I have a stuffed animal that I call Bunny.
When I make her dance, it is very funny!
I got her for my birthday when I turned three.
She is soft and fuzzy and very special to me!
One day I took Bunny in the car to drive all over town.
When we got home, Bunny was gone. I felt very down!
We looked and looked for her everywhere.
In the car, under the beds, and under the chairs!
Finally, my special Bunny was found.
She was in our garage on the ground.

Ava Peeler, Grade 2
Bramlett Elementary School, GA

Our U. S. A.

Oh USA we pledge our hearts to you
Truthful and deep
We love you
From the salty seas
To the beautiful rain forest
We love you
From the soft green grass
To your leaves on the trees
We love you
Our people, our land
We will always protect you
Because we love you

Justin Davis, Grade 2
Kerr Elementary School, OK

About My Cousin

I like my cousin.
Her name is Katelin.
Her clothes are nice.
Sometimes we get in fights.
Her shoes are nice.
I know where she lives.
I don't know the street name.
I miss her over the weekend.
I know she watches *I Carly*.
On the bus she always saves me a seat.
Sometimes I sit with her.
She is my sister's cousin too.

Shannon Harris, Grade 3
Alpena Elementary School, AR

Fall

In fall, tall trees
Have leaves.
It's cool in fall.
I like fall.
Fall is fun.
We lay
In bed all day.
Leaves change colors.
They fall down.
When they fall down,
They are found.
That's why I like fall!

Arden MacDonald, Grade 2
Eagle's View Academy, FL

Grandparents

G od-loving
R eally fun
A ntique shopper
N ice
D oes things with me
P al
A wesome
R eally grateful
E normously fun
N atural antique lover
T alker
S alsa maker

Claire Lowe, Grade 3
Clinton Christian Academy, MO

Diving

Springing, plunging into the depth.
A massive rumble of thunder
Evaporating into clouds of water.
Afterwards, deafening silence.
Surfacing, the sun's rays
Seem to pull themselves away.
As I break,
The water gently laps.
The cicadas sing.

Ella Zodrow, Grade 2
Crafty Ladies Home School, FL

Christmas

C andy canes left by Santa
H appy holidays to all
R elatives come on Christmas day
I ce falls off the roof
S nowmen are all around our house
T rees are covered with ice
M istletoe hangs for kisses
A ngels fly all around our house
S tockings are filled with toys

Savannah Heindel, Grade 2
Doyle Elementary School, LA

My Grandparents
They are so bright they are like the stars in the night.
I love them so much they are like a dove.
They have been in my heart from the start.
When my grandfather died my mom cried and I said it's ok.
I will always remember them all my life.
They are as sweet as meat.
They brighten my heart from the start of everything
I've known them my whole life
They're as sharp as a knife
They are the sweetest people in the world.

Seth Pugh, Grade 3
A H Watwood Elementary School, AL

The Chase
The fawn lays in the field, waiting for its Mom.
The cheetah is waiting for just the right moment to...
POUNCE!!!!
The fawn fled.
The fawn is mumbling to itself, flee, flee!!!
The cheetah is catching up to the fawn.
The fawn sharply turned...
SLAP!!!!
The cheetah ran into a tree.
The fawn escaped.

Savana Stampler, Grade 3
Camden Station Elementary School, KY

Friendship
F un
R eliable
I ncredible
E nchanting
N eat
D urable
S incere
H elpful
I mportant
P recious

Matias Ostrowicz, Grade 3
Virginia A Boone Highland Oaks Elementary School, FL

I Am a Tree

I am a tree,
I am your friend.
I am old,
I am new.

I am growing
just for you.
I help you breathe,
I help you grow,

And sometimes
I make you think:
How I grow,
what's inside me,
And maybe you
will never know.

I know about me
and I know about you,
And that is good enough
to make my life grow.
Lucas Gabrovic, Grade 3
Sabal Point Elementary School, FL

Memory

As you walk in,
greeted by…happiness,
all your sadness goes away.
Just the joy,
makes you gleam with happiness.
Candy apples,
with caramel glaze,
on shelves stacked high…
as if it were an 8 foot tall
person on the wall.
Chocolate sweet,
gumdrops and Sour Patch
goofys everywhere.
Get a candy tube
filled with…
sweet, sugary, sour powder,
in every candy dispenser.
That's what…
I'll remember
from that memory…
in that bracelet.
Riley Walker, Grade 3
Camden Station Elementary School, KY

Ice Cream!

cold sweet
creamy
it
slowly
d
r
o
p
s
on
to
the
floor and
there is
no
more
Grant Evans, Grade 3
Camden Station Elementary School, KY

The Crash

At my friend's house
Set up the ramp
Rode my bike down the hill
The whole way down
Air zooming thru my hair
Like a chainsaw
I did a nose wheelie
I ramped I…
Crashed!
Landed on my face
Hurt so bad
I felt like water
In a waterfall
Zooming down the Rocky River
Crying like rain
Bleeding like fire
Tyler Breneman, Grade 3
Buckner Elementary School, KY

Memories About Grandpa, Dad, and Mom

Memories are precious
because they are pretty thoughts
in my mind.
I remember my grandpa
telling me a bedtime story,
my dad giving me a bath
and scrubbing my back,
and my mom going out of town
making me sad.

Elijah Jackson, Grade 2
Lee A Tolbert Community Academy, MO

Rainbows

Some rainbows have red,
Some rainbows have green
With all the colors in between.
Rainbows are high with clouds below;
The leprechaun found the pot of gold.
Some come with rain or some come with sun;
I think rainbows are so much fun!
Rainbows are a promise from God,
To love and protect us and keep us from harm.

Gracie Wong, Grade 2
Briarwood Christian School, AL

My Sneaky Cat

My sneaky cat is white as snow.
For show and tell I brought her to school whatcha know.
She went there and everywhere.
She even went behind Miss Flammang's purple chair.
When I let her go in the house she pounced on the couch.
When I went to my room she ran too!

Lily Martin, Grade 3
Cool Spring Elementary School, NC

My Dream

I like to play baseball.
It's a fun sport to play.
One day I will be a famous pitcher
with many fans who will come watch me.
That is my dream and it will come true someday.

Tyriq Rhodes, Grade 1
Oakland Primary School, SC

Sports
Playing
Yelling
Cheering
Running
Pitching
And having fun!

Sarah Swan, Grade 2
Ponte Vedra Palm Valley Elementary School, FL

Fall
Leaves crunching under my shoes,
Look at all those colors,
Orange, red, yellow, and brown,
Swirling through the air,
Landing at my feet,
On a cool, autumn day.

Abby Priebe, Grade 3
Hunter GT Magnet Elementary School, NC

Snow
Snow falls it sparkles all the way to the ground.
Crunch crunch crunch goes the snow.
Someone shouted out snow ball fight…
then snow flies everywhere
then the kids were covered in snow
so they went home and drank hot cocoa.

Noah Guy, Grade 3
Camden Station Elementary School, KY

My Wish
I made a wish long ago very long ago I would not dare to tell a soul but I would
think you would know. I walk down the street very quiet I listen to the only sound
crying, I kept walking faster and faster it stopped. I kept walking down the quiet
street very quiet and lonely.

Madison Bond, Grade 3
Charles Towne Montessori School, SC

Trees
Trees are beautiful.
Trees put a smile on my face.
Do not kill the trees.

Darrah Shannon, Grade 2
Virginia A Boone Highland Oaks Elementary School, FL

Lemonhead!

Lemonhead Lemonhead.
Your sourness is sweet.
Your taste is outstanding.
You feel hard in my hand.
How do you do it?
You taste so good!
I want more Lemonheads.
Because you taste so good!
When I chew you I say SOURER!

Dylan Porter, Grade 3
Camden Station Elementary School, KY

God's Love

I love the birds singing.
I love crickets croaking.
I love the people and God.
I love the things He made.
We love you.
More and more.
I love living things.
It's made from You.
You love us.

Thomas Phillips, Grade 3
Alpena Elementary School, AR

Friendship

Annaclaire
wise, humble
jumps, cartwheels, cheers
you can make it!
Annie

Mary Michael Thames, Grade 3
Briarwood Christian School, AL

Lemons

L emonade on a hot summer day
E veryone takes a break to sip and
M akes a sour face
O val full of juice and seeds
N ot so sweet but tart and tangy
S unny yellow fruit

Matthew Grinnell, Grade 3
Norris S. Childers Elementary School, NC

Bentley Stroud

Bentley
athletic, outgoing
track, wakeboarding, basketball
I invite friends over
Pouky

Eliza Cannon, Grade 3
Briarwood Christian School, AL

All About Max

Max
funny and truthful
video games, boxing, football
I like being loyal
D.J.

Jon Houston Seibert, Grade 3
Briarwood Christian School, AL

All About Jackson

Jackson
funny, smart
skimboarding, soccer, reading
he is always considerate
Jack-attack

Brianna Brown, Grade 3
Briarwood Christian School, AL

All About Julss

Julia
funny, short
swimming, gymnastics, football
I include other people
Julss

Jillian Barfield, Grade 3
Briarwood Christian School, AL

All About Alexandria

Alexandria
goofy, nice
gymnastics, swinging, climbing
loyal to other people
Alex

Mivi Briley, Grade 3
Briarwood Christian School, AL

Emily

Emily
Compassionate, tenderhearted
Swimming, ballet, spelling
I love helping others
Emmy
Emily Waddell, Grade 3
Briarwood Christian School, AL

Me!

Libby
Artistic, smart
Reading, drawing, playing
Very kind to others
Libbyloo
Libby Neal, Grade 3
Briarwood Christian School, AL

Chris

C ool
H ungry
R isky
I s my friend
S even.
Cristian Salazar, Grade 1
Evangelical Christian School, TN

Pumpkin

Pumpkin
Orange, Halloween
Eating, glowing, carving
Pumpkins glow brightly
Pie
Zane Wilson, Grade 3
Doyle Elementary School, LA

My Friends

David
Funny, friendly
Pitching, batting, running
Kind to my friends
Kelly
David W. Scharf, Grade 3
Briarwood Christian School, AL

Football

Football
Brown, white
Running, jumping, catching
Touchdown means everything
Ball
Cade Breland, Grade 3
Doyle Elementary School, LA

All About Me

Nick
Funny kids
Hiking, playing, drawing
Having fun with friends
Nini
Nick Badolato, Grade 3
Briarwood Christian School, AL

Christmas Spirit

Christmas
Present, generous
Holiday, merriment, excitement
Here is a Christmas tree
Jolly
Kathy Nguyen, Grade 3
Nesbit Elementary School, GA

Roxxey

Roxxey, my dog,
We have so much fun!
I threw a ball.
It went under a log.
I lost the ball!
Logan Foody, Grade 1
Evangelical Christian School, TN

Ms. Cookoo

My least favorite teacher is Ms. Cookoo.
When I first met her she said, "Moo!"
I thought she was crazy,
When she called me lazy.
I wonder what to do when I'm through.
Anna Zhong, Grade 2
Spoede Elementary School, MO

Brianna's Log

Brianna
Happy, fun
Skating, swimming, cheerleading
Always kind to others
B
Jackson Stubbs, Grade 3
Briarwood Christian School, AL

Holiday

Holiday
Scary, weird
Walking, knocking, ringing
A weird holiday
Halloween
William Ivy, Grade 3
Pottsville Elementary School, AR

All About Me

Kinsey
Honest, silly
Riding, reading, swimming
Kind to my friends
Nicole
Kinsey Harris, Grade 3
Briarwood Christian School, AL

Garden Snake

Garden snake
Green, long
Eats mice, slithers, lays eggs
It is very fun.
Reptile
Spencer Wagoner, Grade 3
Clinton Christian Academy, MO

Pearl's Job

Pearl
Picks
Purple
Prickly
Pinecones
Laci Woods, Grade 3
Pottsville Elementary School, AR

Bugs

Bugs are little cute and fluffy
Caterpillars are soft and fluffy
And beetles are creepy and crawly.
Lots of bugs are creepy and crawly
And lots of bugs are soft and fluffy.
But all of them are cute and squirmy.
But none of them are ugly and disgusting.
Landon Wright, Grade 2
Evangelical Christian School, TN

Smart or Stupid

What's more fun?
Home or school?
I rather home,
But I want to be clever.
I guess I'll do homework.
There must be something fun
About these spelling words!
Connor Goudeau, Grade 3
Caneview Elementary School, LA

Sunny Day

The sun is shining out,
So don't stay in and pout.
Go and have a wonderful day,
So then you can sway.
Have fun, but don't run,
Just jump around and play,
So you can keep a smile on today!
Delaney Jones, Grade 2
Evangelical Christian School, TN

Cookies

Cookies, cookies
I love cookies
Sugar cookies
Chocolate cookies
Oatmeal cookies
I love cookies
Sweet and tasty.
Sydney Tuthill, Grade 1
Cool Spring Elementary School, NC

Angel

A lways nice to us
N ever mean to us
G ives faith
E xcellent at everything
L oving

Pierson Waite, Grade 2
Macon-East Montgomery Academy, AL

Ice Cream

Ice cream, ice cream
I love ice cream
Chocolate
Vanilla
I love it so much.

Gianna Diaz, Grade 1
Cool Spring Elementary School, NC

Santa

S anta says Ho Ho Ho!
A lways jolly,
N ever sad,
T otally glad,
A nswers letters.

Brentson Cox, Grade 2
Macon-East Montgomery Academy, AL

Being Kind to Others

Rebekah
freckles, goofy
tennis, piano, swimming
is kind to others,
Bekah

Harrison Gauldin, Grade 3
Briarwood Christian School, AL

All About Eliza

Eliza
pretty, funny
horseback-riding, swimming, running
I'm kind to others
Liza Loubu

Bentley Stroud, Grade 3
Briarwood Christian School, AL

I Am Creative

Jay
Resourceful. playful
Scouting, playing, helping
Being kind to friends
Jay-Bird

Jay Kynerd, Grade 3
Briarwood Christian School, AL

All About Me

Ryan
Kind, Christian
Playing, singing, napping
Be nice to others
Buggy

Ryan Tripp, Grade 3
Briarwood Christian School, AL

I Love Me

Erika Johnson
Smart, Christian
Singing, swimming, scrapbooking
Being kind to others
Ladybug

Erika Johnson, Grade 3
Briarwood Christian School, AL

Midnight

She is black and white.
She is lazy.
She can be wild too.
She likes to give hugs and kisses.
Most of all I love her.

Jacob Norman, Grade 1
Cool Spring Elementary School, NC

The Butterflies

The butterflies can fly.
They land on plants.
They fly everywhere.
They fly away from you.
The butterflies change color.

Faizon K. Taylor, Grade 1
Oakland Primary School, SC

People

People are smart
Some are not
People run fast
Some cannot
People tell lies
Some tell the truth
Good things happen
And bad things do too.

Lily Smith, Grade 2
Kerr Elementary School, OK

The Mystery Of ?

Here I am dropping on Earth.
When I stop
a rainbow transforms in.
I help the environment.
I can look silver,
surprise children
and get their feet wet.
The rain forest was named after me.

Irvin White, Grade 3
Lee A Tolbert Community Academy, MO

My Hair

My hair is thick,
I like it thick.
I think my hair is cute.
I have so many hairstyles,
Like braids, afro puffs, and plaits.
I wish I had other hairstyles.
I like "My Hair" because
it is CUTE and FABULOUS.

Sydney Tillman, Grade 3
Rowan Elementary School, MS

Barracuda

Barracuda
dangerous, long
diving, biting, eating
gray, fast
Barracuda

Steven Lessard, Grade 1
Guardian Angels Catholic School, FL

We Decorate Our Christmas Tree

Christmas is celebrating Jesus,
We decorate our Christmas tree.
I do the bottom part,
My mommy and daddy help me.
When it gets cold we run around,
We eat Christmas cookies, too.
We drink hot chocolate,
What do you like to do?

Isaac Gray, Grade 1
Westlake Christian School, FL

I Like to Spend Time with My Family

Christmas is a special time of year,
I like to spend time with my family.
We make Christmas cookies,
We pick a Christmas tree.
We decorate it with candy canes,
I like to eat them, too.
We decorate with ornaments,
That is what we like to do!

Gracie King, Grade 1
Westlake Christian School, FL

Cloud

The white, marshmallowy cloud
In the bright, blue sky
Sings like a bird
In the morning light.

The brown, fluffy cloud
Is a bunny
Prancing in the sunny meadow.

Katelyn Rivers, Grade 3
Wellington School, FL

Starfish

Starfish
small, bumpy
crawling, squeaking, hiding
pink, cute
Starfish

Amelia Johncola, Grade 1
Guardian Angels Catholic School, FL

Weekends

Weekends are cool,
we have no school.
Weekends are great,
we get to stay up late.
Weekends are fun,
we get to play in the sun.
Weekends are neat,
we get to go out to eat.
Weekends are a breeze
I get to do whatever I please.
Mondays come too fast.
The weekends never last.

Will Paschal, Grade 2
Westminster Christian Academy, GA

Grandparents

G reat
R yan lover
A wesome
N ice
D onut lover
P al
A lso fun
R adiant
E ager
N eat
T alker
S hopper

Ryan Pitts, Grade 3
Clinton Christian Academy, MO

Shoes

My mom has shoes,
She loves shoes.
She says that she
doesn't have many.
I looked and saw
shoes, shoes everywhere!
On the wall
On the bed
Oh my shoes!

Ariel Fowler, Grade 3
Alpena Elementary School, AR

Halloween Monsters Everywhere

Scary Halloween, menacing ghosts
Scary Halloween, weird skeletons
Scary Halloween, gross goblins
Scary Halloween, obnoxious monsters

Trick-or-treat!

Scary Halloween, torturous devils
Scary Halloween, mask killers
Scary Halloween, unusual aliens
Scary Halloween, freaky jack-o'-lanterns

They're horrible,
They know you're out there,
You just have to wait!

Drake Crosby, Grade 3
Buckner Elementary School, KY

My Horse

Horse horse
Come to me!
We will get some horse ice
Cream.
Oh don't you worry it just looks
Like something you like!

My! I love you, my horse
You are just for me!
I love you my horse so much!
My horse!
I will not step on your foot
I love you my darlin' horse
I cannot be without you
My horse!

Emily Moore, Grade 3
Hillsdale Christian School, OK

A Starry Night

Some wind is blowing
All stars are shining brightly
The moon is glowing

Matthew Prosser, Grade 3
Lowcountry Day School, SC

Thirsty Leopard

Leopard lapping water from a leaning ladder pail.
Now he goes on home and drinks some water from his throne!
Now he is tired and goes to bed
He dreams of laughing leopards instead.
He wakes up in the morning by noon
And gets some breakfast very soon.
He is very thirsty after that, so goes to the stream for a little lap.
He says, "I am thirsty little stream, please give me some water."
And the stream says back, "Well drink me up you old cat!"
The leopard does what he is told. The stream says,
"Thank you, and please send the rain, for me and to help grow the grain."
Thirsty, thirsty leopard!

Emily Long, Grade 3
Hillsdale Christian School, OK

Brooklyn

Missing her I wish I could see her again.

Crying in my bed dreaming about her
Wishing I could see her again.

We live far away wishing I could see her again.
I am lonely wishing I could see her again.

Playing with her but now I can't.
Wishing I could see her again.

Brooklyn

Braelynn Cotton, Grade 3
Buckner Elementary School, KY

Imagine a Day...

Imagine a day...
when you spend your day at a sandy beach
swimming in the shiny, shimmering ocean,
drinking pink lemonade with lemon and
a silly straw with it and
laying down on your towel
getting a nice tan.

Imagine a day.

Lindsey Crites, Grade 3
Robert E Lee Expressive Arts Elementary School, MO

Animals
I love animals
Because they are beautiful.
When I see them,
They make my heart cheerful.

I like the cat,
Because it is so sweet.
Also, I like the cardinal,
It knows how to tweet.

When I grow up,
I want to be a vet.
To help animals,
I know I will never forget!
Jennifer Vargas, Grade 3
G E Massey Elementary School, NC

Powerful Papa
I think of you like a dove
My heart is filled with all your love
When my heart is broken in half
You always make me have a great laugh

When we read the book of Psalms,
You always hold me in your palms
You always played games with me
And you always watch me climb a tree

When we listen to some jazz
We do the dance move spazz
See you in heaven, and remember
I love you!
Levi Jones, Grade 3
A H Watwood Elementary School, AL

The Mother of Nature
Once upon a time
there was a girl who lived in the forest
with the spiders and bees.
She sang beautiful songs,
but she was invisible.
She helped Mother Nature
to protect the treasures
of rain, soil, and sun.
She was warm and left her home
three times a day,
morning, evening, and midnight
to check on her children
and guard them from fires,
ice ages and people who litter or steal.
Precious Love, Grade 2
Lee A Tolbert Community Academy, MO

St. Nick
St. Nick is a jolly old fellow
With a belly that shakes like Jell-O!
He comes so quietly to your house
Like a sneaky little mouse.

He doesn't want you to see him
So turn off all your lights!
He'll leave you a toy
That will bring so much joy.

Once he's done
With his busy night
He's off to the North Pole
And out of sight!
Zachary Williamson, Grade 3
Carver Elementary School, NC

The Blue Sky
The white clouds moving in the air
And now the white clouds
Turning into gray clouds
The rain begins to fall
The puddles form
Grant Newton, Grade 2
Buckner Elementary School, KY

Jumping in the Sea
I had to go under the sea,
I saw a big shark being mean.
A dolphin passed by,
Like it soared through the sky,
And that's what was seen by me.
Aaron Xavier, Grade 2
Orlando Junior Academy, FL

The Angel

A lady sings
For the king
She goes to the store after she sings
To buy a ring
For the king
The lady's wing
Flies
Up in the sky
(She was an angel!)
Somer Crnkovic, Kindergarten
Northeast Baptist School, LA

The Bubble

I got in a bubble,
I went to get a double bubble.
I went past a dog,
I went past a frog.
I went on the pond,
and I floated on the water.
I saw a big fish.
Then I floated off,
and went home.
Austin Carter, Grade 3
Cool Spring Elementary School, NC

Brian

Brian
loving, kindness
cub scout, swimming, basketball
always believe in God
B.C.
Brian Cabrera, Grade 3
Briarwood Christian School, AL

Night Lights

Stars are bright.
They light up the sky
Like firecrackers
On the Fourth of July.
They are like the sun
At night.
Chelsea Francis, Grade 3
Caneview Elementary School, LA

Winter Wonderland

The crunchy snow
Falling from the sky
Slurping the cocoa
The Christmas shows come on and
Everyone gets a cozy feeling
While sitting by the sizzling fireplace
Putting up the Christmas tree
While beautiful snowflakes
Slowly start falling
To the ground
Playing in the snow
brrr
It's a beautiful
Winter Wonderland
Nathaniel Crowe, Grade 3
Buckner Elementary School, KY

I Am a Penguin

I am a penguin,
As cute as can be.
I am always there,
But nobody can see me.

All of my friends
Always say "Hi,"
But five seconds later
They say "Good-bye."

I'm cute when I cuddle,
And I'm fun to watch
When I sit in a puddle,
And everyone always loves me.
Catherine Arthur, Grade 3
Sabal Point Elementary School, FL

My Dad

My dad loves me.
My dad plays with me a lot.
My dad runs with me outside.
My dad takes care of me when I'm sick.
That's why he is my dad.
Rimani Stuckey, Grade 1
Oakland Primary School, SC

Pankake
Patrick
fast, funny
biking, running, rip-sticking
playing games with friends
Pankake
Patrick Moore, Grade 3
Briarwood Christian School, AL

Joanna
Joanna Files
flexible gymnast
drawing, baking, riding
not lying to friends
JoJo
Joanna Files, Grade 3
Briarwood Christian School, AL

All About Me
Caleb
soft, loving
acting, dancing, playing
playing with best friends
Bug
Caleb Alford, Grade 3
Briarwood Christian School, AL

Austin
Austy
funny, loving
play, running, singing
nice, sweet, play sports
Posty
Austin Laatsch, Grade 3
Briarwood Christian School, AL

Chaney
Chaney
artistic, funny
biking, reading, dancing
always encouraging my friends
bookworm
Chaney Eller, Grade 3
Briarwood Christian School, AL

All About Me
Sarah
Funny, athletic
Swimming, cheering, drawing
Playful with her friends
Punky Brewster
Sarah M. Singleton, Grade 3
Briarwood Christian School, AL

Just About Me
Sally Grace.
Funny, silly
Running, reading, subtracting.
Make my friends laugh.
Silly face!
Sally Grace Sullivan, Grade 3
Briarwood Christian School, AL

Being Funny Is What It's All About!
Sam
hyper, funny
knitting, drawing, riding
being funny to others
Sami bo bami fe fi fo fami
Sami N. Martin, Grade 3
Briarwood Christian School, AL

Me
Joseph
funny, flexible
whistling, camping, launching
loving them all time
José
Joseph Harper, Grade 3
Briarwood Christian School, AL

About Me
Collin
Athletic, energetic
Shooting, hitting, reeling
Don't tell on people
Susie
Collin L. Dorrill, Grade 3
Briarwood Christian School, AL

The Mean Boy
There is a mean boy
Who rides my bus.
He always makes the driver fuss,
(Fuss, Fuss, FUSS!)
He yells and screams, and makes lots of noise,
For us girls and boys.
He throws bunches of paper
Into the air;
And last week on Monday,
His pencil landed in my hair!
I turned back toward him
And with a quick yell,
"You'd better stop it,
Or I will tell!"
When he is absent,
It is very nice.
Everyone cheers;
Some even cheer twice!
We all know this bully-free day won't last,
It goes by too quickly,
Just entirely too fast.

Kelsey Champagne, Grade 3
Caneview Elementary School, LA

Thanksgiving
I'm thankful for the food we have to eat.
Thankful for my nose and I'm thankful for my toes.
I'm thankful for books. Thankful for the animals.
Thankful for ME! I'm thankful for people.
Thankful for the math we do.
I'm thankful for the friends I have. I'm thankful for games.
And I'm thankful for the bathroom. And I'm thankful for our table.
I'm thankful for the colors and I'm thankful for pictures.
And teachers and songs and TV and stickers.
I'm thankful for the kitchen.
I'm thankful for the poems and birthdays.
And all the people we love.
And God. And the bible.
The money and the clothes we have. And the toys and chairs.
I'm thankful for the smells we have. And the tastes.
I'm thankful for a car and I'm thankful for the grass.

Jada Edwards, Grade 2
Robert E Lee Expressive Arts Elementary School, MO

Math

Subtraction is my passion.
Just wait until I put it into action!
Now I see in my vision
there is division.
Next, I will study multiplication
on my vacation.
I am in position
to practice my addition.

Cameron Hellgeth, Grade 3
Landmark Christian School, GA

Fall

It is fall.
I see a ball.
I want to play.
Stay out of the way!
I see a bike.
I want to hike.
I'm going to school.
I'm jumping in my pool.

Hunter Warren, Grade 3
Eagle's View Academy, FL

Santa Eats Our Cookies

Santa Claus gives us presents,
I saw Santa at the mall.
He was asking us what we wanted,
I asked for a princess doll.
The reindeer come down the chimney,
They leave carrot crumbs on the floor.
Santa eats our cookies,
Then he likes to soar.

Sarah Burkart, Grade 1
Westlake Christian School, FL

My Bike

I like to ride my bike
I like to ride it on base
My bike has four wheels
Two wheels are for training
I love my bike

Aaralyn Sasser, Grade 1
Oakland Primary School, SC

Cookies for Santa

Santa gives me presents,
He gives me lots of toys.
He puts them under the Christmas tree,
He gives them to girls and boys.
We make cookies for Santa,
They are green, brown, and red.
I make them with my mom,
"They look good!," I said.

Kaitlyn Rodriguez, Grade 1
Westlake Christian School, FL

Snowballs and Cookies

I like throwing snowballs,
We roll down a big hill.
You can go sledding,
It is a big thrill.
You get presents from Santa,
Santa has reindeer.
We leave him cookies,
Christmas is near.

Hudson Sanders, Grade 1
Westlake Christian School, FL

Brothers

B oring
R otten
O vereat
T oo icky
H ave bad taste
E very day they're a pain
R ude
S o mean

Tracy Munsterman, Grade 3
Lakeland Elementary School, MO

The Zoo

The zoo seems pretty fun!
I like the zoo.
The zoo has animals.
Tigers like to run.
The zoo is cool.

Leilah Rivera, Grade 1
Oakland Primary School, SC

Shimmering

Small stone peeking out
From all the others
Smooth as a water glass
Sharp as the tip of a fork
I can see through it so clearly
Like it's transparent
One shimmers in the sunlight
Like all the others
But some way amazingly different
Motionless but special
The hot flaming sun
Makes it feel bumpy and warm
A cloud covers the sun
A shadow cast itself
Across the shimmering stone
It's all dark
The cloud moves on
The sun reveals itself again
The stone sparkles
As if it was flashing a wink at me
With a twinkle in its eye
Stephanie Edds, Grade 3
Buckner Elementary School, KY

The Colors of the Rainbow

Red
Nice, deep, rich
And thick

Yellow
Bright, joyful
A sign of light and happiness

Green
An outside color
The color of grass
A sign of a pretty day

Blue
Deep, soft,
Creamy, soothing
The color of the sky

Violet
Soft, nice, creamy
Rich
Allie Whitmire, Grade 3
Westminster Christian Academy, GA

The Ride

Going on a Mountain
Ready to start moving
Up the tall steep hill
Finally at the top
As nervous as a cat
In a room full of rocking chairs
My heart about to pop
ZOOM, WHIZ, ZIP
Down and up
Left and right
Not an animal in sight
Moving as quick as lightning
We are finally stopping as slow as cats
Getting off
My heart rapidly pounding
Finally Thunder Mountain is done
Devin Swinney, Grade 3
Camden Station Elementary School, KY

I Love Pumpkins

Pumpkin young,
Pumpkin old,
Pumpkin orange,
Pumpkin sold.
Pumpkin carved,
Pumpkin seed,
Pumpkin stem,
Pumpkin teeth.
Pumpkin pie,
Pumpkin fluff,
Pumpkin bread,
Pumpkin stuff.
Pumpkin scary,
Pumpkin fright,
Pumpkin light,
In the night.
Cheyenne Willis, Grade 1
Ava Elementary School, MO

The Rain

The rain is a pit-pat on the roof.
Like a clip-clop of a horse's hoof.
The rain is a lullaby for me.
Like the beautiful buzzing of a bee.
The rain is falling on my head.
It makes me want to go to bed.
I love the rain.

Makenna McElwee, Grade 3
Many Elementary School, LA

My Rule

If you mistake it
you can't remake it
yes, that's my rule
if you break it
you can't retake it
if you try to
you won't make it.

Cassie Lopez, Grade 3
Kerr Elementary School, OK

My Trains

I like trains
Trains are fun
Slow trains
Fast trains
Long trains
Short trains
I like trains.

Noah Pharr, Grade 1
Cool Spring Elementary School, NC

God Made Us

God made us kind.
God made us small and tall.
God made us in His perfect love.

God made us love Him.
God made us have a great life.
God made us in His perfect love.

Kyra Heavner, Grade 3
St Paul's Lutheran School, OK

May in the Sun

Summer is great!
Free of school;
Vacations start.
Getting to the beach;
Running, splashing, building sandcastles.
Fun in the sun.
Summer is the best!

Lucah Broussard, Grade 3
Caneview Elementary School, LA

Optimus Prime

My pumpkin is strong,
But he can't beat Megatron.
He thought he needed the cube,
But that would kill him,
Because it's too powerful!
Do you know why he is strong?
Because he is Optimus Prime.

Jacob Taylor, Grade 3
Coral Springs Elementary School, FL

My Pumpkin Wizard

He's mine, all mine.
He's a wizard!
Come near him, he'll zap you.
When he flies, it will make you cry.
Why?
I really don't know.
Do you?

Anthony Saint-Cyr, Grade 3
Coral Springs Elementary School, FL

The Dog and the Cat

The dog played.
He played and he played.
He stopped.
He sees a cat.
He likes the cat.
The cat likes the dog.
They played.

Nathaniel Roberts, Grade 1
Oakland Primary School, SC

You Shine Like a Shining Star

You shine like a shining star,
Yet so I think you are.
You twinkle in the night sky,
And others seem to not know why.
The planets orbit around the sun,
There's not two, there's only one.
I wonder what it would be like to be a star of my own,
I'd shine and twinkle in the sky and I know I'd really be shown.
Would a star ever fall down
Into a city or a town?
What would I do if I were a star?
Would I paint pictures or travel far?
I want to become a star someday,
Basically I'd be shouting HOORAY!
Hooray, hooray what a wonderful day.
You're like a little diamond in the sky,
Up in the bright night sky up high.
You shine like a shining star!

Katharine Mehle, Grade 3
Columbia Catholic School, MO

Love of a Grandparent

My grandparents light up a very sad day,
They support me in a very good way,
They make me say Hooray on birthdays,
They love me a lot and they support me too,
Wow! so many things my grandparents do!

They welcome me on Christmas parties,
I love it when they give me smarties,
They let me use a lot of things,
So wonderful it makes me sing

On Christmas, they give me lots of things,
Like books and magazines,
That have pictures of lots of things.
They listen to me reading, and also when I'm singing
They love it when I make speeches, one thing I would love to say
I love my grandparents in every way.

Tanija Swain, Grade 3
A H Watwood Elementary School, AL

Tyler Ward

T remendous
Y oung
L oyal
E nergetic
R esponsible

W itty
A thletic
R espectful
D ashing

Tyler Ward, Grade 3
Virginia A Boone Highland Oaks Elementary School, FL

Imagine a Night...

Imagine a night with your big sister
buying a cake with her name and cheese pizza for her party
and going swimming.
Waiting for her friends and cousins to come to eat the pizza
and play fun games.
Then eating cake and going to bed by watching the Grinch
and going to sleep.
Then making breakfast for yourself.
Then waiting for parents to pick everyone up to go home.
Imagine a night.

Kiessence Edwards, Grade 3
Robert E Lee Expressive Arts Elementary School, MO

School Daze

If you had to pay a fee
I know no kid would get a "D"
A little study is key
If you want to get a "C"
Just do more homework, it seems to me
And you might just get a "B"
Listen to your teacher is what I say
And you're bound to get that "A"
What really counts if you want to be cool?
Is doing your best, when you go to school!

Paul Chafetz, Grade 3
Virginia A Boone Highland Oaks Elementary School, FL

My Cats

I have two cats,
One is mean,
Another is nice and funny.
The mean one hisses
when she sees the nice one.
One is funny because
she likes to act crazy.
I love them both.

Nelina Rodriguez, Grade 2
Cool Spring Elementary School, NC

Cloud

The big, fluffy cloud
In the light, blue sky
Floats like a boat
In a crystal, clear lake.

The tiny, white cloud
Is a cotton ball
Rolling in bright, green grass.

Amanda Gregoire, Grade 3
Wellington School, FL

I Try to Catch Santa Claus

My family comes over for Christmas,
We open presents and play.
The elves make cool toys,
It is a very special day.
I try to catch Santa Claus,
I stay up in the middle of the night.
My brother helps, but we never catch him,
He flies out of sight.

Olivia Schick, Grade 1
Westlake Christian School, FL

Clownfish

Clownfish
tiny, orange
jumping, swimming, eating
striped, bright
Clownfish

Luke Pero, Grade 1
Guardian Angels Catholic School, FL

Cloud

The white, puffy cloud
In the clear, blue sky
Danced like a giant butterfly
In the night.

The slow, bumpy cloud
Is a gator
Walking to its home.

Alex Fox, Grade 3
Wellington School, FL

Helping

I like to help with my family
most any time
I like to help my teacher
when she needs something done
She gives me fun learning games
That's her way to help
and then I help my friends
because everyone needs help sometime

Hue Yang, Grade 3
Kerr Elementary School, OK

I Like Singing Christmas Carols

I like hearing stories about baby Jesus,
My brother reads to me at night.
I like singing Christmas carols,
I like Christmas trees with lots of light.
Santa Claus rides on a sled,
He flies to my house very fast.
He gives me awesome presents,
I really have a blast!

Christina Karalis, Grade 1
Westlake Christian School, FL

My Birthday

My birthday is July the 14
that's the best day of the year
I get presents on my birthday
my birthday is a really long day and
it is very fun, I love it.

Maniya Dawson, Grade 1
Oakland Primary School, SC

Kara Samuels

I am a little girl and I love to play,
I hear beautiful music each and every day,
I see my family, they are my very best friends,
I wish I was in Heaven, where the crime problem ends.

I feel happy and safe when I am with my family,
I feel frustrated when I have C's on my report, though rarely.
I get angry when I am asked to sing!
I am puzzled when Mommy tells me I will lose my blessing.

I dream about going to Heaven…ummmn.

I wonder if I will go to Heaven, oh when will this be?
I plan to see my angel, but Jesus I really want to see,
I hope I will go to Heaven and be with my Jesus,
I know I will be in God's arms, I feel very anxious.

I understand that God loves me and I love Him too,
I learn that God is real, you can learn this too,
I value my friends, family, and really God, I pray to Him on my knee,
I love my God and His angels, go love Him too, just feel free,
I am afraid of the devil, and from him I always flee.

Kara Samuels, Grade 3
Berea Jr Academy, SC

Flowers

April showers bring May flowers
Flowers need water every day
In spring we plant flowers
The seed of the flower makes it grow
When I plant a flower, I feel terrific
A flower can be any size or shape
The color of a flower looks pretty
The smell of a flower smells like beauty
Flowers are beautiful
A flower makes me smile
The stem of the flower makes me feel strong
Flowers are like humans
Flowers die like humans do
Frost makes the flowers die,
While the sun and water helps the flowers stay alive.

Ashley Logan, Grade 3
G E Massey Elementary School, NC

Snow

Snow, snow
falling down,
down to the ground
as soft as a kitten
as cold as an iceberg
Snow, snow everywhere
Making snowballs
and a lot of snow
to share
Making snowmen
for hot, hot
chocolate
with tasty
marshmallows
in cold, cold pockets
Taking warm showers
Laying in warm beds
watching snow glow
like lightning strikes
ZING, ZANG,
ZONG, ZOOM.

Myha Stricker, Grade 3
Camden Station Elementary School, KY

Dogs

Out of all the animals
Dogs are the best.
They are better
Than all the rest.
They can be
Big, medium, or small.
But, it doesn't matter —
I love them all!
They are so cute
When they drool.
Dogs are
So cool!
Sometimes they're nice.
Sometimes they're not.
But it doesn't matter —
I still like them a lot!

Aubrie Cimino, Grade 3
Eagle's View Academy, FL

Hot Steamy Days

Walking into the hot steamy salt water
I'm getting farther and smaller,
Soon my mom will think I'm a mouse
I will hear the waves crashing down,
But then...
SPLASH!!
I am forced to go underwater
Like a lion chasing a zebra,
I'm with the lion on the waves
Then the lion gets the zebra,
I start to get a little slower
Lion chewing,
I make a stop.
When I come back
I see like...
One million people,
Just sitting there,
I will hear mom say
Over here Alex!!
I'm wondering when will I be back.

Alex Faulk, Grade 3
Camden Station Elementary School, KY

Good-bye Great-Grandma

My great-grandma is gone
She always had fruit punch
And cookies waiting for us
Her wrinkly fingers in her lap
As she's laying in the bed
My great-grandma is gone

Her eyes closed
My aunt calls us
Crying going on like
A small lost child
My great-grandma is gone

My face droopy and red
Bursting tears going down my face
Like a little baby that wants its mom
My great-grandma is gone

Brenna Denham, Grade 3
Camden Station Elementary School, KY

You and Me Forever

I love you
You love me,
'Cause we are a family
Every time I see you,
You make me giggle happily.
Every time I play hangman,
You always get me

Every time I pick a flower,
It's like your face on the
Flower smiling back at me
You are like a pot of gold
In my heart,
You will always hold
You are like a gold mine,
Full of beautiful gold

When you are gone,
It rains all day
But when we are together,
It clears up right away
I love you forever
You are my Sunshine!
Nautica Swain, Grade 3
Childersburg Elementary School, AL

Camp Rock

Camp Rock has a girl.
Camp Rock has friends.
Camp Rock has guitars.
Camp Rock has stars.
Camp Rock has music notes.
Camp Rock has kisses.
Camp Rock has tears.
Camp Rock has hearts.
Camp Rock has butterflies.
Camp Rock has rings.
Camp Rock has a lake.
Camp Rock has designs.
I like Camp Rock
Because it has things!
Kira Rymer, Grade 2
Bostian Elementary School, NC

Fall

When it is fall
The leaves fall off
The tall brown tree.
They are bright,
Shiny red, yellow,
And green.
Squirrels come
With acorns.
They get the
Red, yellow, and green leaves.
I raked them up.
I like fall!
Meg Hall, Grade 2
Eagle's View Academy, FL

My Elephant

He didn't squirt at anything,
A snake
A toad
A toucan
A monkey swinging tree to tree
A black and yellow buzzing bee
A giraffe
A lion
A hyena
A toucan red and green and blue,
He squirted because he wanted to.
Georgia Bond, Grade 1
Blessed Sacrament School, FL

I Want a World Where...

I want a world where...
I am as nice as an angel.
I am pretty as a butterfly.
The desk calls me to learn.
My mom is as beautiful as a rose.
My family are colorful flowers.
The moon sings to me.
My friend shines like the moon.
My dad is as sweet as a cherry lollipop.
I want a world where...
Suntoria Benjamin, Grade 3
Rivelon Elementary School, SC

All About Me
Sarah
Nice, kind
Dancing, singing, riding
Likes to have fun
Sage
Sarah Gail Harrison, Grade 3
Briarwood Christian School, AL

Natalie
Natalie
funny, super
ballet, swimming, softball
friends love each other
Nat Nat
Natalie Nandwa, Grade 3
Briarwood Christian School, AL

Mac
Mac,
funny, glasses,
tire swing, reading, swing,
funny, nice, has friends, patience,
big Mac
Katy Bi Watson, Grade 3
Briarwood Christian School, AL

The Friendship
Cole
Funny, kind
Football, soccer, basketball
Helps people when hurt.
Colebean
Ashley Russell, Grade 3
Briarwood Christian School, AL

Ward
Ward
playful, funny
tennis, hunting, video games
makes people laugh a lot
weird
Riley Travis, Grade 3
Briarwood Christian School, AL

Do the Job Right
Carrie
nice, playful
cheerleader, swimmer, sports
respect to all people
Carebear
Cole Williford, Grade 3
Briarwood Christian School, AL

All About Me
Madison Wright
Caring, funny
Shooting, flipping, cheering
Funny to my friends
Maddie
Madison R. Wright, Grade 3
Briarwood Christian School, AL

A Day with a Friend
Harrison
Freckles, funny
Running, soccer, reading
Fun to be around
Big H
Rebekah Pylant, Grade 3
Briarwood Christian School, AL

Dreamer
Morgan
Silly, flexible
Running, swimming, climbing
Always silly with friends
Josie
Josie Benson, Grade 3
Briarwood Christian School, AL

Durden
Durden
Kind, sweet
Soccer, skiing, football
Always trust in God
Dur-Dur
Durden Duell, Grade 3
Briarwood Christian School, AL

Cats

C is for collar.
A is for animal.
T is for tail.
S is for Skittles.

Kenna Gray, Grade 1
New York Elementary School, MO

I Wish

I wish the Canes would win the cup.
I wish I'd get a pup.
I wish I had a chocolate cake.
I wish I could bake.
I wish I wish I was a Super Hero.

Johnathan Korkie, Grade 3
The Fletcher Academy, NC

Mississippi and Oklahoma

I live in Oklahoma,
but my friends live in Mississippi.
Oh! How I love my friends
Who live in a spiny, tiny, little city
in the state of Mississippi

Zach Reding, Grade 3
Alpena Elementary School, AR

School

School is fun.
School is cool.
You learn new things
    every day!
I like school.

Ashlin Usrey, Grade 2
Alpena Elementary School, AR

Fall

In the fall
Leaves fall.
In the fall
Leaves fall from the tree.
Leaves fall.

Ethan Sapp, Grade 2
Eagle's View Academy, FL

Gongs Are Cool

G olden and black
O bject it is
N oisy and loud
G rand it is…good for
    waking up people.

Wyatt Higginbotham, Grade 1
Evangelical Christian School, TN

All About Trinity

Trinity
silly, tall
gymnastics, hip-hop, swimming
being kind to others
Trinny

Joseph Dickinson, Grade 3
Briarwood Christian School, AL

Things About Me

Jordyn
Funny, loving
Swimming, playing, writing
Helpful to my friends
Monkey

Jordyn Fuller, Grade 3
Briarwood Christian School, AL

A Book About Me

Mason Reid Algren
Hyper, funny
Playing, puzzling, gaming
Nice friend to others
Macy

Mason Reid Leland Algren, Grade 3
Briarwood Christian School, AL

Puppy

P is for popcorn.
U is for under.
P is for paw print.
P is for pooch.
Y is for yawn.

Benjamin Hollon, Grade 1
New York Elementary School, MO

Sky
The sky is high.
Birds fly in the sky.
Stars twinkle bright
In the moonlight.

Ally Ratner, Grade 2
Virginia A Boone Highland Oaks Elementary School, FL

The Pigs
Pigs like to lay in mud at the farm.
Pigs can splash in the mud.
Pigs like to play in the mud with another pig.
Pigs like to eat!

Mason Doane, Grade 1
Oakland Primary School, SC

The Little Lamb
The little lamb was hiding in the backyard
and he found a lamb and
they wanted to play.
The lambs are happy.

Trinity Alston, Grade 1
Oakland Primary School, SC

Smiles
I smile cute when my mom and dad say they love me.
I smile scared when I am in the dark.
I smile tired when it is time to go to bed.
God smiles at me when I teach my little brother to pray.

Emma Guenther, Grade 1
Guardian Angels Catholic School, FL

Smiles
I smile cute when my mom tickles me.
I smile loving when my mom and dad snuggle with me.
I smile funny when my dad pushes me in the pool.
God smiles at me when I sing to Jesus.

Lindsey Dobson, Grade 1
Guardian Angels Catholic School, FL

My Dad

My dad is a giant.
He has lots of clients.
My dad loves to eat velvet cake.
But he doesn't like snakes.
He likes the color yellow
But he's not mellow.
He is funny
And he has lots of money.
My dad is strong
And he doesn't like to be wrong.
Blaine Chaney, Grade 3
G E Massey Elementary School, NC

My Colorful Pumpkin

My colorful pumpkin is big and round.
One day, I colored it,
And it made me spin around!
I may also cry,
Since I don't want her to die.
My pumpkin also likes to eat cherry pie!
My pumpkin likes its personality,
Because she likes her shape and size.
She doesn't like to scare people,
Because she's not that kind!
Marissa Crea, Grade 3
Coral Springs Elementary School, FL

The Fox

The fox was in the box
He couldn't get out
'Cause it was locked

The clock tick-tocked
The fox put on some socks

A wolf knocked
On the box
And put on long knee socks
Santana Pierson, Kindergarten
Northeast Baptist School, LA

Little Star

My little bright star
shining in the dark black sky
following me home.
Emily Goss, Grade 2
Roseland Park Elementary School, MS

Elk

The brown furry elk
walking in the scary woods
searching for his friends.
Hunter Grantham, Grade 2
Roseland Park Elementary School, MS

The Blue Butterfly

The blue butterfly
in the dark, blue large sky
playing a flying game.
Chloe Taylor, Grade 2
Roseland Park Elementary School, MS

Shining Stars

The stars are shining
in the dark sparkly sky
twinkling in the night.
Zoe Rohrbacker, Grade 2
Roseland Park Elementary School, MS

The Friends

I love my friends
I love to play with my friends
All day long
Mariela Torres, Grade 1
Riverhill School, AL

Butterfly

Fly butterfly to the zoo
See a bee
Then fly home.
David Austin Wood, Grade 1
Oakland Primary School, SC

Halloween Night

Pumpkins, pumpkins everywhere,
There's enough for us to share.

Every Halloween night,
Pumpkin's light is very bright.

Pumpkins, pumpkins everywhere,
There's enough for us to share.

Jack-o'-lanterns shout "Boo!"
Owls are hooting "Who-o-o!"

Pumpkins, pumpkins everywhere,
There's enough for us to share.

Kids in costumes yell, "Trick-or-treat,"
They never say, "Smell my feet!"

Pumpkins, pumpkins everywhere,
There's enough for us to share.
Ryan Melnick, Grade 2
Spoede Elementary School, MO

My Family

My family lives in Tennessee.
There are 3 of us.
We share hermit crabs.
We do agree.
And still we are a family.

Our hair is brown.
Are eyes are blue and green.
Our skin is pretty, too.
We're all that we can be;
That's why I love my family.

We laugh and play,
We work and be quiet,
We see each other every day.
The world's a good place to be;
Because, we are a family.
Kaiya Grice, Grade 1
Byrns L Darden Elementary School, TN

My Little Sister's Cat

My little sister had a cat
This little cat was really fat
The cat ran away
but it came back to play
We played in the back yard
Alayna Aurora Silvania, Grade 1
Oakland Primary School, SC

Hot Wheels

My Hot Wheel is fast
When it goes on the track.
Hot Wheels look cool.
Hot Wheels are fast
When you step on the gas.
Tyree Evans, Grade 1
Oakland Primary School, SC

Autumn

My sister Autumn is funny
She is so pretty,
She makes me laugh so hard.
I love Autumn so much
She loves me.
Ainsley Ashley, Grade 1
Oakland Primary School, SC

All About Ellie

Ellie
nice, goofy
soccer, football, swimming
nice to other people
Ellbell
Drew Schroeder, Grade 3
Briarwood Christian School, AL

Andrew

Andrew
nice, grateful
runs, swings, plays
what are you doing?
Porkchop
Andrew Ponder, Grade 3
Briarwood Christian School, AL

Time with My Mommy

You are so nice
You are so sweet
You are the perfect Mommy
To me

You are like an angel from heaven above
You play games, watch TV, and even crack a
Pistachio nut for me

You're like a diamond mine
Filled with beautiful diamonds of
Blue, orange, yellow, pink, brown, purple, red
Robin egg and sky blue, gold, and silver like
A rainbow in the sky
Sent from Jesus
You are a perfect Mommy
Because you spend time
With me

Madison Hobbs, Grade 3
Childersburg Elementary School, AL

Christmas Night

While the parents and children are in the cozy bed
Snuggled up tight
Warm as the sun in the summer,

The night is as quiet
as an owl flying in the dusk.

The night is as cold as a glacier.

The night moon shines a spotlight on the floor
Like a flashlight shining on the stage.

The night is as black as burnt coal,
The air is as cold as when you first open a freezer...

And when you wake up
You scream, "PRESENTS!!!"
To the entire family.

Weston Graham, Grade 3
Camden Station Elementary School, KY

Fall Leaves
Colorful fall leaves outside.
Millions and millions!
Shhzstwvaanw.
Cold air.
Really cold wind hitting my arms.
Kinda happy.
Tyler Cox, Grade 2
Buckner Elementary School, KY

Red
Apples are red,
twisty ties and shoes.
I know that books and bags
are red, some birds
and if I make a wish on red,
it will come true.
Donnisha Kelly, Grade 3
Lee A Tolbert Community Academy, MO

The Christmas Night
It is Christmas night,
And the Christmas lights are bright.
Jolly Old Nick,
Slid down my chimney brick.
I'm glad he came,
Are you glad he came?
Parker Whittle, Grade 2
Macon-East Montgomery Academy, AL

November Is Cool
November is cool
We celebrate Thanksgiving
We run and play
and eat good food
We are thankful for friends
Life is good
Llemile Palacios, Grade 3
Kerr Elementary School, OK

Dogs
Dogs
Dislike
Dumb
Doormen
Blake Andrews, Grade 3
Pottsville Elementary School, AR

The Bed
There was a little boy named Ned
He sat in the bed
He fell out of the bed
And turned red
Logan King, Kindergarten
Northeast Baptist School, LA

Family
My family can help me.
My family loves me.
My family takes care of me.
I love my family.
Taylie Griffiths, Grade 1
Oakland Primary School, SC

Cats Like to Play
There was a cat named Annabel.
She likes to play with her mom.
She has orange fur.
She has gray paws.
Hannah Duncan, Grade 1
Oakland Primary School, SC

Purple
Purple looks like a basket.
Purple tastes like grapes.
Purple smells like perfume.
Purple feels like a nice shirt.
Christopher Rochette, Kindergarten
Oakland Primary School, SC

Thanksgiving

I love Thanksgiving because
They have candy and pie and apples
And all kinds of things!
And we get to play
And we also get to sing and dance
And I feel like my heart is moving
So sweet!

Aya Bellaoui, Grade 2
Robert E Lee Expressive Arts Elementary School, MO

Zachary

Z ealous
A thletic
C reative
H appy
A rtistic
R esponsible
Y outhful

Zachary Winer, Grade 3
Virginia A Boone Highland Oaks Elementary School, FL

Pencil

Always there if you need him
Always handsome and sharpened
Always in that very same place
You know a pencil can't be replaced
Shiny and skinny
You know you want me because I can write and draw
JUST GET ME OUT OF THIS STORE!!

Sam Mattingly, Grade 3
Camden Station Elementary School, KY

Peaceful and Danger Nature

The wind is as fast as a cheetah
and the leaves are tumbling like a boulder.
and the trees are falling like a giant's foot
thomp
thomp
thomp
the animals as wild as a boxer.

Evan Hartmann, Grade 3
Buckner Elementary School, KY

Tommy the Turkey

Once there was a turkey that lived on Thanksgiving day.
He hollered and he howled which was rude they would say!
The silly, silly turkey would swim in the sea.
He would like to jump the waves — just like you and me!
In early November, he escaped to wiggle his toes in the sand.
Instead of sticking around to get eaten by a Pilgrim hand.
With the seagulls, Tommy the turkey would hang out.
And go fishing, build sandcastles, and go all about.
Tommy the turkey has been going to the ocean for five years.
So, he doesn't have to shed tears.
This is how Tommy the turkey has saved his life,
So, he doesn't get carved by a Pilgrim knife.

Ashlyn Rhyne, Grade 3
S Ray Lowder Elementary School, NC

Me

Luke
Fun, silly, creative
Son of Rob and Renu
Who loves art, math, and books
Who needs water, food, and shelter
Who feels happy, friendly, and good
Who gives love, hugs, and gifts
Who fears heights, clowns, and ghosts
Who would like to see Australia, Asia, and Magic Man
Who dreams of school, art, and Legos
Who lives in Columbia
Olson

Luke Olson, Grade 2
Robert E Lee Expressive Arts Elementary School, MO

Soccer

Soccer is the sport I mostly like
Soccer is the game of my life

Running, running with all the effort
Showing, screaming with joy
I made the winning goal!

Soccer is the best of all
Soccer is way better than the mall

Tomer Shkori, Grade 3
Virginia A Boone Highland Oaks Elementary School, FL

Star Sister

She's the world
I hear big laughter
in the living room.
I look left
then I look right…
I look down.

It's the princess
laughter of Rosie.
She's laughing
at a cartoon.
Like Tom and Jerry,
Loony Toons.

She's an angel.
She's a fairy princess
flying free
She is an amazing girl.
She's the world.
Phillip Hazlett, Grade 3
Camden Station Elementary School, KY

Leaves

Soaring through the
Sky
Gently reaching out
To the
Surface
Touching the
Ground for the
First time
Screaming in happiness
Eee!
As they form a
Pile

As I run
Faster and faster
To the pile of leaves
Jump
Crunch!
Matthew Guy, Grade 3
Camden Station Elementary School, KY

Cedar Point

Going every way you can,
Side to side,
Hearing wind whistling,
Through the soft almost silent breeze.
Trying to find your pick,
Riding rides,
Sprinting swiftly,

So you can find the roller coaster,
Millennium force,
Second largest and humongous
Roller coaster there.
As you feel like trees are touching you
High above ground

As it blasted at 93 mph,
Zooming past like a rocket,
Screaming as you plummet
To the surface,
The bank turn,
You can't feel it,
Comes to a complete stop,
As you say you conquered it.
Jacob Brizendine, Grade 3
Buckner Elementary School, KY

Christmas Cheer

Shining lights among the tree
everybody's filled with glee,

because they see upon the star
that Baby Jesus is our guard.

Your mother's cooking a feast to share
with your families everywhere,

all because of that little star
Baby Jesus is sleeping far.

God bless the world
everybody!
Sam Pena, Grade 3
Camden Station Elementary School, KY

The Christmas Angel
There was an angel who was small,
I bought her at the mall.
I loved her so,
She even made my heart glow.
She is pretty and funny,
I would not trade her for money.
Allison Parson, Grade 2
Macon-East Montgomery Academy, AL

Halloween
When I say Halloween,
You say ooh.
When I say boo,
You say boo too.
I love trick-or-treating
On Halloween.
Cheran Dixon, Grade 1
Oakland Primary School, SC

Pecos
Horses are pretty.
I like horses.
My Gammy has a horse
named Pecos.
I like to ride him.
He is my friend.
Aubryanna DuFrene, Grade 1
Oakland Primary School, SC

The Toy Car
I have a favorite car that's special to me
It gives me a lot of glee.
It sparkles a lot
and gets really hot.
I know Santa gave it to me
because he left it under the tree.
Bradford Nickles, Grade 2
Macon-East Montgomery Academy, AL

Bakugans
I like bakugans.
I have twelve of them.
I have red ones and all colors.
On my birthday I hope to get a lot more.
Michael Long, Grade 1
Oakland Primary School, SC

I Plant a Seed
I plant a seed
to watch it sprout
if I see weeds
I will pull them out.
Jaice Calderon, Grade 1
Oakland Primary School, SC

Dogs and Cats
Dogs are cool.
Cats can claw.
Dogs wag their tails.
Cats like to sleep.
Sarah-Jane Hamilton, Grade 1
Oakland Primary School, SC

Flowers
The flowers are beautiful.
I like to smell them.
Butterflies like to smell them too.
I want to pick some for my teacher.
Jameera Edwards, Grade 1
Oakland Primary School, SC

My Daddy
I love you Daddy.
I miss you Daddy.
You are my angel.
My sweet daddy.
Lauren Smallwood, Grade 1
Oakland Primary School, SC

Black

Black is a juicy olive.
Black is like the clouds on rainy days.
Black is the dark sky at night.
Black is a scared cat at Halloween.
Black is my dark shirt.
Black is my dad's very dark hair.
Harrison Mitchell, Grade 3
Evangel Christian Academy, AL

Ollie

I have a cat.
He runs a lot.
He sleeps at night.
Ollie enjoys his mom.
Ollie enjoys his family.
Noah Williams, Grade 1
Oakland Primary School, SC

Dogs

Dogs are fast.
Dogs are smart.
Dogs can hunt.
Dogs can run and jump.
Dogs make good pets.
Desmond McMillan, Grade 1
Oakland Primary School, SC

The Creation

God made the sky,
the plants and animals
He created us
and the big sea too.
He also is our best friend
Steven Bradley, Grade 1
Oakland Primary School, SC

Thankful

I thank you, Lord, for the blue sky above;
I thank you, Lord, for people I love.
I thank you, Lord, for this good food.
Thank you, Lord; I'm in a thankful mood.
Harrison Bourg, Grade 2
Briarwood Christian School, AL

Halloween

H aunted house is scary
e A ting lots of caramel apple candy
L ots and lots of candy
L ots of yummy treats
O n Halloween night
W e dress up really scary
w E trick or treat all night
w E go and we are sad
N o more Halloween.
Saira Richardson, Grade 3
Columbia Catholic School, MO

Baseball at the Mall

I went to the mall.
And guess what I saw?
A baseball on the wall.
Run the bases y'all!

I reach but I fall.
For help I call.
I need to be tall
To play basketball.
Ryan Larkins, Grade 2
Briarwood Christian School, AL

What Is Your Problem?

What is a bag?
What can you do?
Can you do something?
Can you answer that?
What is a rose?
Annabelle Colon, Grade 1
Oakland Primary School, SC

To Giggle and Laugh and Play

Sunflowers are yellow, like the sun.
But can't you see, it's so much fun.
To play and laugh and giggle too.
To have so many fun things to do.
Then you know there's just no hate.
But can't you see, there's so much great!
Palmer Strubhar, Grade 1
Stone Ridge Elementary School, OK

I'm Talking My Birthday!

I'm talking my birthday!
I'm talking birthday party, presents!
I'm talking birthday cake, seven candles, make a wish!
I'm talking balloons, birthday hats, birthday plates, birthday napkins!
I'm talking birthday piñata, hit it with a bat, candy falls out, "Hooray!"
I'm talking birthday cards, gifts in wrapping paper, purple ribbon, open them up, get out the toys, say "Thank you!"
I'm talking my birthday!

Isabella Leddy, Grade 1
Blessed Sacrament School, FL

Flying

Soaring
Smiling
Landing
Running
Jumping
Fluttering

Flying

Zachary Chattaway, Grade 2
Ponte Vedra Palm Valley Elementary School, FL

Fall

Orange, yellow, red, and brown leaves falling down,
Down to the ground,
Crackling and crunching leaves,
The sound reminds you of fall.
Cool air fills the world so nice,
Mixed with all the leaves and smells,
Pumpkin pie and pumpkin bread with cinnamon,
Yum!

Austin Roberts, Grade 2
Wellington School, FL

School

Reading, math, science
Learning, teaching, testing
Fun, happy, excellent!

School

Brooklyn Pattison, Grade 2
Ponte Vedra Palm Valley Elementary School, FL

Lizard

There once was a lizard named Peck
He also had a long long neck.
He was so thin.
He looked like a pin.
I always see him on my deck.

Priyansh Pilly, Grade 2
James E Sampson Memorial Adventist School, FL

Bo Jackson

Bo Jackson
fast, nice
runs, tackles, and snaps
cool, good sportsmanship, awesome player
Bo Bo, Bo Jackson

Chan Holt, Grade 3
Briarwood Christian School, AL

Isaac

I mportant
S uper
A wesome
A stonishing
C ool

Hilel Guberek, Grade 3
Virginia A Boone Highland Oaks Elementary School, FL

Laughing

I like to laugh. I don't like to cry.
When I laugh I think about the sky.
When I cry I start to sigh.
When I play I start laughing and when I'm laughing I am gasping.
It's so fun to laugh when you take a bath.

Daiten Fontenot, Grade 2
Doyle Elementary School, LA

Cheering

I like to cheer and make it fun
I like to be number one.

So stand on your feet and lets go cheer
Let's yell and yell so all can hear.

Kiyanna Gayle, Grade 3
James E Sampson Memorial Adventist School, FL

Apples

Apples are pretty.
Apples are red green and yellow.
They are juicy and sweet to eat.
A special treat for me.
Apples are good.

Aaliyah Murray, Grade 1
Oakland Primary School, SC

Halloween

We eat candy.
We dress up in costumes.
We carry candy buckets.
We cut scary faces into pumpkins.
We light them up after dark.

Louis Wright III, Grade 1
Oakland Primary School, SC

Dalmatians

Dalmatians are white with black spots.
I think Dalmatians are beautiful dogs.
Dalmatians like to play.
Many Dalmatians help firefighters.
I want a Dalmatian.

Todd Odell, Grade 1
Oakland Primary School, SC

Grandmas

Grandmas are good.
Grandmas never get mad.
Grandmas are cool.
Grandmas give grandkids good toys.
I love my grandma.

Robert McConnell, Grade 1
Oakland Primary School, SC

Apples

Apples are red, yellow, or green.
Apples are good.
Apples are shiny.
Apples are healthy.
Apples are perfect!

Anevay Aguilar, Grade 1
Oakland Primary School, SC

My Clown Pumpkin

My pumpkin is a clown.
He does not own a hound.
He owns a small car.
If you make him mad,
He will squirt you with his nose.
He will be nice,
If you buy him
An ice cream cone!

Kishan Rampersaud, Grade 3
Coral Springs Elementary School, FL

The Doggone Analogies Test

That doggone analogies test,
Made my brain go west,
It made my desk,
Become a big mess,
Then my mom made tea,
In a big pot for me,
And it was a bad day,
For me to go and play.

Daniela Martinez, Grade 3
Nesbit Elementary School, GA

Jesus' Birthday

We can see angels at Christmas,
They have halos and wings.
They are very pretty,
I love to hear them sing.
Jesus' birthday is on Christmas,
He brings us lots of joy.
Jesus died on the cross,
For every girl and boy.

Sawyer Amende, Grade 1
Westlake Christian School, FL

The Little Gallito

"If I eat I'll dirty my beak
and I won't be able to go
to the wedding of my Tio Perico!"
But he could not resist.
He ate the corn, and dirtied his beak.

Gustavo Martinez, Grade 1
Oakland Primary School, SC

Basketball

Playing basketball is so fun.
When I run around outside
I get lots of excitement from being in the sun.
Making three-pointers and shooting hoops
makes me feel like I'm running loops.
I also get a lot of excitement when I play on the courts
that's why basketball is my favorite sport.

Tyliq Laws, Grade 1
Oakland Primary School, SC

Halloween Night

Spooky scary,
Getting candy,
Saying BOO!!
Walking far
Getting home
Bed time.
Lights out!!!

Peyton Thompson, Grade 2
Ponte Vedra Palm Valley Elementary School, FL

Winter

I like the snow.
It's fun to sled!
A snowman's fun,
With a hat on his head!
Throwing snowballs is lots of fun!
I throw them at my dad
In the bright, bright sun!

Lauren Brown, Grade 1
St Vincent De Paul Elementary School, MO

Homework

Homework, homework, I hate homework.
I forgot to do it and remembered at night.
Oh my gosh, I'm having such a fright!
I picked up my pencil there is no lead.
I guess tomorrow I'll have to act very, very dead.
Oh, wait you say tomorrow is Saturday.
Ok, I'm fine today.

Andy Banks, Grade 3
Columbia Catholic School, MO

You
When I see the sky
I think about you
When I see the sun
I remember you
When I look at the water
I see you
When I look at myself
I can't live without you!

Sebastian Fernandez, Grade 3
Virginia A Boone Highland Oaks Elementary School, FL

I Can Never See Him at Night
Santa Claus gives me a lot of presents,
He flies all around with his reindeer.
I can never see him at night,
Even though he flies so near.
On Christmas morning I wake up,
I wait for my mom and dad.
We're excited to open the Christmas presents,
My brothers and I are glad.

Yianni Bakkalapulo, Grade 1
Westlake Christian School, FL

Christmas
Christmas is coming
I'm already humming
It is so pleasant
That I'm getting presents
Cookies and cakes
I just can't wait
I love meeting my family and friends
Too bad Christmas has to end

Eric Marcos, Grade 3
Virginia A Boone Highland Oaks Elementary School, FL

Lunch
There once was a snake in my lunch.
And my stomach did grumble a bunch!
A treat would be nice.
I'll even take ice.
So I ate the snake with a crunch!

Isaac Fan, Grade 3
Hunter GT Magnet Elementary School, NC

Danger
Catastrophe
Exaggerate
Running
Screaming
Calling for help
Dad! Mom!
Daddy Shark
Mommy Bear
ANGRY!!!!!!
Plan B is...
RUN!!!!!!!!!!!!!!!!!!!!

Alanna Perrin, Grade 3
Hunter GT Magnet Elementary School, NC

Toby and Bella
Toby is playing tug of war with Bella
I watch them go back and forth
While I sit on the smooth couch
They run to the kitchen
I wonder what they are doing
I get up and walk to the kitchen
While they look at the pantry
"Do you want a bone?" I ask
I get the bone out of the pantry
They go under the sofa and eat their bones
Toby and Bella are great friends together

Madi Sullivan, Grade 3
Buckner Elementary School, KY

China
Imagine a day in China...
that you ate famous foods that are very good and yummy.

Imagine a day in China...
and you saw girls wearing very beautiful dresses,
and you can't take your eyes off of them.

Imagine a day in China...
that everybody is eating very yummy treats and you are too.

Imagine...China...again.

Lisa Zhou, Grade 3
Robert E Lee Expressive Arts Elementary School, MO

Football Is Awesome

Football is awesome
But you can get really hot.
Football is cool
And I like it a lot.
My dad always says, "Do good in the game,"
And we always win as the same.
I think you should try it
Because you will like it.
It's really fun
And I play it a ton.
Football is my favorite sport
But I still like the basketball court.

Joseph Welch, Grade 3
Evangelical Christian School, TN

The Proud Pumpkin

Pumpkins are very sweet to eat!
But I don't eat pumpkins.
Because I have a pet pumpkin.
When my pumpkin gets sad,
It is not pretty. It throws a fit.
When she gets sad, she is not proud.
So I try to cheer her up!
Sometimes though it does not work.
I bring her favorite food: Mac and Cheese!
Then she gets so happy she bursts with color!
When she is so, so tired of changing colors,
She falls fast asleep.

Julianna Citrangulo, Grade 3
Coral Springs Elementary School, FL

Tennessee

T remendous
E xcellent
N ice
N ature
E normous
S pecial
S uper
E xciting
E njoyment

Jake Kurkin, Grade 3
Virginia A Boone Highland Oaks Elementary School, FL

Santa

I love reindeer,
They are very sweet.
They look pretty,
I will give them a treat.
I love presents,
Santa surprises me.
He gives me presents,
Under the Christmas tree.
Sophia Mahaz, Grade 1
Westlake Christian School, FL

Hearts

Hearts beat
And pump the blood
God made them
So we could have life
Beautiful and wonderful.
Without them
We could not live.
Isn't God good?
Kayli Perry, Grade 3
Tri-County Christian School, MO

Cloud

The lovely, huge cloud
In the cute, blue sky
Shuffled like a merry cat
In a quiet house

The kind, gorgeous cloud
Is Mrs. Koehler
Walking in the garden.
Brandon Watson, Grade 3
Wellington School, FL

Christmas Lights

I like when Santa comes to our house,
He comes down the chimney.
He leaves us lots of presents,
He leaves them under the tree.
We decorate the house,
We put on the Christmas lights.
They look beautiful,
I like to see them at night.
Mike Malagies, Grade 1
Westlake Christian School, FL

Christmas Colors

Christmas colors are red and green,
They are very bright.
I love how they look,
Especially at night.
We open a present on Christmas eve,
We always stay up late.
We put out food for the reindeer,
We can't wait!
Delaney Welch, Grade 1
Westlake Christian School, FL

He Sneaks in the House

The reindeer can fly to my house,
They come on Christmas Eve.
They are big and brown and eat carrots,
After they deliver every present they leave.
Santa has a long white beard,
He sneaks in the house while we're asleep.
He has red clothes and a black belt,
He will never make a peep.
Grace Cropper, Grade 1
Westlake Christian School, FL

The Ball

Bounce bounce the ball.
Up and down the hall.
Big ones, little ones.
Red, blue, green and white.
All on one ball.
Joseph Pommell, Grade 1
Oakland Primary School, SC

Pumpkins

pumpkins
spicy, fruity
nutty, sweet, salty
round, orange, spooky, big
thump, boom, thud, knock, squish
Annie Swaters, Grade 3
Lakeland Elementary School, MO

Rain

I love the
         rain.

Rain,
    Rain,
       Rain.

It never gives you a pain
   in the back.
It's just water.

            The sound of
                        rain
            is very beautiful.
            It's a good
                        Sound machine, too.

It looks like crystals
            falling
                from
               the sky.
        Rain is a miracle.
        and God is, too.

Avery Sepesi, Grade 2
Westminster Christian Academy, GA

Softball

I'm calling all of ya'll
To come play softball.
All you need is a bat and a glove.
I'll tell you about a sport you'll really love.
You hit the ball and run, run, run.
It's really lots of fun!
While others are trying to get you out
All your fans scream and shout!
We try to win
Until the very end.
So, grab your stuff —
These teams are pretty tough.
Meet me on the field
Where friendship and sportsmanship is what we build!

Alexis Morrison, Grade 3
Norris Childers Elementary School, NC

Raindrop

It looks like a tiny blue piece of sky
Falling from above.
It sounds like the wind
Since it's going so fast.
It feels like a tiny waterfall
On my skin.
It tastes like water exploding
On my tongue.
It smells like the sweet wet watery
Smell of the ocean.
Finally it hits the ground
Splashing everywhere!

Emma Merlini, Grade 2
Ponte Vedra Palm Valley Elementary School, FL

Where I'm From

I am from spaghetti.
I am from pizza at Domino's.
I am from McDoubles from McDonald's.
I am from Clue, Monopoly, and Andy Griffith Mania.
I am from football my favorite team is Chargers.
I am from Cruz — for three years.
I am from Brock. I have known Brock for three years.
I am from Ms. Fisher — for two days.
I am from Westbrooks for 1 year.
I am from home — 2 years.
I am from Bat Wing Bush hogging I love it.
I am from a flat bed truck.

Canaan Scruggs, Grade 3
Alvaton Elementary School, KY

Gum

Tastes good
It's chewy
Love it
It is
The best
In the
Whole world

Gum

Walker Wells, Grade 2
Ponte Vedra Palm Valley Elementary School, FL

I Am From…

Domino's pizza hot and spicy. McDonald's chicken nuggets yummy and crunchy.
Wal Mart's cupcakes cold but delicious and full of ice cream. McDonald's french
    fries crunchy steamy hot and salty.
Baked cookies chocolatey crunchy but good. Computer games fun funny and
    playful.
Piczo sending messages playing with glitter and listening to music videos.
The board game Monopoly playing with stick people and racing.
Contests staring at people hopping on one foot but having a great time.
Outside catching lightning bugs putting my hand up high and catching bugs who
    light up their butts.
Reading books and reading big words. Coloring pretty pictures using crayons and
    having fun.
Playing with Linzey chasing each other and having a playful time. Me and Eliza
    acting like twins and making friendship.
Me and Caylie reading together and exercising. Me and Caitlyn making jokes and
    giggling a lot.
Me and Sophie making tricks and doing gymnastics. McDonald's cooking and
    making orders.
New York in a hotel watching TV and having a nap. The mall shopping for jewelry
    and having fun.
School writing and working and glad to be with my teacher. Barbies saying hello
    and being nice to others.
My Barbie computer playing games speaking Spanish. Racing fake hamsters
    running and jogging.

Hannah Hagan, Grade 3
Alvaton Elementary School, KY

I Wonder*

Sometimes I just sit and wonder what the earth was like a million years ago.
Did giant spiders rule the earth? Were deserts filled with snow?

Did the brontosaurus exist? Did the sky contain sun or mist?

Sometimes I just sit and wonder what the earth will be like a million years from now.
Will the skies be filled with polluted fog? Will there still be snow to plow?

Will there be life on Mars? Will people visit distant stars?

But mostly I just wonder about today and what I will play!

Aaron Thaler, Grade 3
Virginia A Boone Highland Oaks Elementary School, FL
*Inspired by "A Hundred Years Ago" by Jeff Kinney

Waterfalls
Waterfalls splash me.
Waterfalls are fun to watch.
Waterfalls are cool.

Benjamin Bloch, Grade 2
Virginia A Boone Highland Oaks Elementary School, FL

Rocks
A rock
As pink as a rose

Red green rocks
Shining at me

Tiger Eye rocks
Shifting their colors

White gray rocks
As square as a cube

A rough rock
As bumpy as a tree

Red rocks
As the color of the sun

A gray rock
As the color of the moon

A tan rock
As sandy
As the desert
A black rock as dark as the dark sky

Donovan Schneider, Grade 3
Buckner Elementary School, KY

Summer Is Fun!
Summer is fun!
When the hot air comes,
It is a lot of fun.
We can go outside,
And play our favorite games.

Summer is fun!
When the flowers are here,
And they bloomed in Spring,
They look so very nice.
Oh, so, so, very nice.

Summer is fun!
When you are out of school,
You go to friends' houses,
Or you go on vacation,
Or stay at home and swim all day long.

Summer is fun!
We get to do all kinds of things.
We get to play.
We get to go on vacation.
We get to see friends and meet some, too.

Summer is fun!

Sierra Fisher, Grade 3
St Paul's Lutheran School, OK

Trucks
Some trucks are big,
some trucks are little,
some trucks have pipes,
some trucks have big wheels
but I love them all.

Trevian Douglas, Grade 1
Oakland Primary School, SC

The Chick
The hen is in the barn
The hen is laying an egg
The egg is starting to crack
The chick is hatched
Wait there is another egg

Lauren Phillips, Grade 1
Oakland Primary School, SC

Gymnastics Is Fun!
Gymnastics
sweaty, strong
flips, handstands, jumps
"You can flip Mary!"
tumbling
Mary Snyder, Grade 3
Briarwood Christian School, AL

My Cousin Kayci
Kayci
nice, humble
back flips, flips, cartwheels
"I love you Skylar."
Kay Kay
Skylar Wallace, Grade 3
Briarwood Christian School, AL

Lovely Me
Hannah Grace
Intelligent, humorous
Runs, plays, laughs
That is so cool!
Cutie
Hannah Grace Roden, Grade 3
Briarwood Christian School, AL

Soccer
Soccer
fun, awesome
runs, kicks, throws
very fun and tiring
football
Grant Stanley, Grade 3
Briarwood Christian School, AL

M&Ms
Mary Michael
funny, nice
sings, laughs, dances
really loyal to others
M&Ms
Anna Claire Giffin, Grade 3
Briarwood Christian School, AL

Friendship
Ashley
Nice, funny
Swimming, basketball, gymnastics
Lets people join in
Ashbash
Cole Livingston, Grade 3
Briarwood Christian School, AL

Jon Houston
Jon Houston
silly, smart
swimming, baseball, art
kind and plays fair
Monkey Jon
Max Moates, Grade 3
Briarwood Christian School, AL

Puff Daddy
Cole
funny, athletic
baseball, football, biking
brings other people up
Puff Daddy
Carrie Kwarcinski, Grade 3
Briarwood Christian School, AL

What I Am and What I Like
Katelyn
Friendly, funny
Singing, flipping, biking
Silly to my friends
Katie
Katelyn Croushorn, Grade 3
Briarwood Christian School, AL

All About Nicky
Nicholas
weird, enjoyable
biking, baseball, basketball
thinks of other people
Nicky
Gabrielle Johnson, Grade 3
Briarwood Christian School, AL

In a Bubble

I was in a bubble
Flying through a sky so high,
I looked down to the earth,
I couldn't see the dirt.
I looked down,
I could see Chinatown.
I looked down again,
I saw Australia's den.
I looked up in the sky,
I could see the stars fly by.
I looked down,
I could see my house.
Pop! My bubble burst.
I was back to my normal self.
Jacob Swicegood, Grade 3
Cool Spring Elementary School, NC

Fruit

Fruit, Fruit
I love fruit
Pineapple
Apple
Strawberry
Watermelon
Pear
Plum
Papaya
Blackberry
Fruit, Fruit
I love fruit
So tasty and so good.
Josh Brown, Grade 1
Cool Spring Elementary School, NC

Ice Cream

Ice cream, Ice cream
We love ice cream
Chocolate
Vanilla
Strawberry
Every kind tastes good.
Hunter Wingate, Grade 1
Cool Spring Elementary School, NC

Candy

hard chewy
sweet chocolatey
sugary sour
minty swirly
sticky nice to eat
pretty like the rainbow.
red, orange, yellow, green, blue, purple.
Twizzler swirly like a lollipop.
chocolate melts like the snow.
bubble gum hops in your mouth.
sour Skittles shake your head up
Hershey bars sweet and nice.
jelly beans jumping up and down.
Mike and Ikes make you dance.
airhead blows your head up.
hard chewy
sweet chocolatey
sugary sour
minty swirly
sticky nice to eat
rock candy hard and crunchy
Kali Letcher, Grade 3
Buckner Elementary School, KY

I Am Thankful

I am thankful for my little brother.
His hair is dark black
and he smells like coconut.
His name is Austin.
I appreciate my brother
because we look at TV
and eat popcorn and pudding.
I appreciate myself the most.
I am thankful for my hands
so I can do cartwheels
and for my ears so I can hear
scary stories.
I am thankful for my lips
so I can taste pizza,
my legs so I can hip-hop dance
and for my body so I can wiggle.
Xavier Lou, Grade 2
Lee A Tolbert Community Academy, MO

I Love Christmas

I love Christmas trees,
Christmas trees are green.
They have lots of decorations,
They're the prettiest things I've seen.
On Christmas it snows,
We make snowmen.
We throw snowballs,
We can't wait till then.

Bella Cortes, Grade 1
Westlake Christian School, FL

Cloud

The white, puffy cloud
In the blue, big sky
Swims like a fish
In the blue wavy ocean.

The soft, smooth cloud
Is a bunny
Hopping in the forest.

Nicole Borrelli, Grade 3
Wellington School, FL

Santa Is Magical

Santa Claus gives us presents,
Santa is magical on Christmas day.
Santa's elves are so cute,
Santa rides on his sleigh.
I believe in Santa Claus,
He has gi-normous clothes!
I like the reindeer in the front,
I love his sparkling red nose!

Reese Koster, Grade 1
Westlake Christian School, FL

A Wonderful Season

Roses are pink and white
In the spring.
All the colors look glad.
My mom, too, is happy
As ever she laughs
When I make funny faces.
We both love the beautiful
Colors of spring.

Virginia Granger, Grade 3
Caneview Elementary School, LA

Muddy Converse

Wash my shoes!
Someone…anyone…
Wash my shoes!
Anybody, anyone, someone…
Wash my shoes!

Nobody wants to
Wash my shoes.

B.J. Olivier, Grade 3
Caneview Elementary School, LA

Fall Leaves

In fall,
The trees stand tall.
I love fall.
God made them all.
I love fall.
Yes, I do!
Fall is fun.
Yes, it is!

Emma Stokes, Grade 2
Eagle's View Academy, FL

I Love My Baby Brother

I have a baby brother,
His name is Eli,
I love him very much,
We hug each other,
I like being a BIG brother!

Ethan James Barrera, Grade 1
Oakland Primary School, SC

My Little Kitten

I found a kitten, it is small
it is soft like a cotton ball
it purrs when I pet it
it cries when I leave
the kitten likes me

Isabella Stang, Grade 1
Oakland Primary School, SC

All About Me
Taylor
Happy, friendly
Dancing, cheering, drawing
Nice to all friends
Taylorbug
Taylor Wheat, Grade 3
Briarwood Christian School, AL

Athlete
Bryce
Happy, athletic
Throwing, swinging, kicking
Love playing with friends
Bryce-man
Bryce H. Perrien, Grade 3
Briarwood Christian School, AL

Praying Mantis
Praying mantis
Brownish-green, watchful
Catches spiders, lays eggs, climbs up
It is very scary.
Invertebrate.
Curtis Barrow, Grade 3
Clinton Christian Academy, MO

Sierra
Sierra
Playful, smelly
Disappearing, appearing, barking
Really likes to snuggle
Puppy
Kailyn Manning, Grade 3
Landmark Christian School, GA

About the Holiday
Holiday
Fun, cold
Eating, cooking, making
Tastes good
Thanksgiving
Logan Warren, Grade 3
Pottsville Elementary School, AR

Guin
Guin
nice, strong
playful, hunter, watch TV
likes to play with them
Froe
Mary Morgan Saunders, Grade 3
Briarwood Christian School, AL

Mouse in the House
There's a mouse in the house,
I'll catch that mouse,
That mouse is in a dirty old house.
If I actually catch that mouse,
I'll put it on my sister's doll house.
Christian Bahre, Grade 2
Cool Spring Elementary School, NC

Me
Matthew
Hysterical, hyper
Jumping, throwing, reading
Likes to run around
Bettylou
Matthew McKenna, Grade 3
Briarwood Christian School, AL

Football
Football
Fun, hard
Running, kicking, tackling
Do not give the other team a goal
Game!
Emily Wilson, Grade 3
Doyle Elementary School, LA

Jenna Flannery
Jenna Flannery
Drawing, enjoys playing.
Soccer, tennis, cheerleading.
Think Jenna is an artist.
Little bird.
Cole Scordino, Grade 3
Briarwood Christian School, AL

Halloween

I can see autumn.
I can see dark gray skies above me.
I can see a black cat's eyes gleaming in the dark.
I can see bright costumes sparkling.

I can smell autumn.
I can smell the sweet smell of candy.
I can smell sweaty costume stenches.
I can smell pie in the oven.

I can hear autumn.
I can hear the occasional owl hooting.
I can hear a moaning mummy.
I can hear a distant scream.

I can taste autumn.
I can taste a ripe pumpkin.
I can taste a batch of candy.
I can taste a fresh baked pie.

I don't need to look at a calendar to know it's autumn.

Aditi Katta, Grade 3
The Parke House Academy, FL

My Mom and Dad

You fill the air with sweet melodies!
When I eat your food my taste buds dance like stars!

Your hearts are as soft as cotton!
Your eyes twinkle like Christmas lights!

My mom is as beautiful as flowers!
My dad is as handsome as the moon!
You're sweeter than sweet!
You're smarter than smart!

My mom likes to go to bed,
My dad likes the color red!

My mom likes the color purple,
My dad likes to murple!

Aaron Journey, Grade 3
Camden Station Elementary School, KY

The Owl
Flying   free,
Like an owl,
White, brown, tan,
Large blue eyes,
Like an owl,
Free,
Strong,
Fast,
Having some friends,
Brave and true,
I can stand up,
Just like   an owl.

Catherine Phillips, Grade 3
Hunter GT Magnet Elementary School, NC

Swamp
Light blue sky
Dark green moss
Trees all around me
Its leaves twisting and blowing in the wind

Swamp lonely all the time
Water all around
The beautiful sound of water rushing through the rocks

Light blue sky
Dark green moss
I like wet places like this

Savannah Button, Grade 2
Buckner Elementary School, KY

Land
I am thankful for this land.
It may be clay, it may be sand.
Each brings harvest year after year.
Resources God planted here.

I am thankful for rivers and trees.
Trees for homes and schools.
Rivers that run to the sea.
Because our forefathers fought to keep us free.

Alex Secrest, Grade 3
G E Massey Elementary School, NC

My Stuffed Bear

My stuffed bear and I do everything together.
We will play in all kinds of weather.
Most of the time, the weather is cool.
When it's warm outside, we play in the pool.
I love that stuffed bear, oh yes I do!
I'd hope if you saw him, you'd love him too.

Belle Fluitt, Grade 3
Many Elementary School, LA

Welcome Little One

Welcome little one to the air we breathe.
Welcome little one to the flowers that weave.
Welcome little one to the birds that sing.
Welcome little one to the birds that spread their wings.
Welcome little one to me and you.
I just wanted to tell you that God loves you.

Emily Pogue, Grade 3
Landmark Christian School, GA

Taylor

Taylor
funny, good grades
riding kid motorcycles, teaching his brother, playing football
make friends laugh, sharing with his friends, he loves his friends,
Tater Tot
I like to be special

Phoebe Cooper, Grade 3
Briarwood Christian School, AL

The Frog and the Pond

One sunny day, a frog went to a pond.
The next day, he went to the pond and he caught a fly.
The next day, he got in a boat.
The next day, he floated away.

Eric Gideon, Grade 3
Northridge Christian School, OK

Waterfalls

I love waterfalls.
The rocks are so very cool.
I love butterflies.

Jason Olofsen, Grade 2
Virginia A Boone Highland Oaks Elementary School, FL

The Fake Lake
I once saw a lake
that was blue and cold,
I thought it was real
but I wish I'd been told
that the blue was paint
and it was just a fake lake.

Then I jumped in it
and I turned blue!
Garrison Dabbs, Grade 2
Briarwood Christian School, AL

Fall
Fall is fun.
Fall is right.
Fall is cold
Through the night.
The colors of the leaves are bright.
Red, orange, yellow, brown.
My family and I
Do not have a frown.
I love fall.
Ava Sheetz, Grade 3
Eagle's View Academy, FL

A Boy Named Jack
Jack was seven years old.
He lived on a farm.
He had a dog named Jeff.
He had a brother named Mark.
Jack said to Mark, Let's go play.
Reginald Morrison, Grade 1
Oakland Primary School, SC

Chicago
Chicago a very busy city
day and night big sounds
honk
honk
people going home from a very busy day
coming back to another very busy day
Dylan Hackney, Grade 3
Buckner Elementary School, KY

The Holy Star
The holy
bright
star

Shines in the silent sky

All
bright
and yellow

The star
Has been flickering
For a while

Its comforting brightness

Makes
Me
Smile.
Emily Powers, Grade 3
Landmark Christian School, GA

Sunset Beach
Hot sand
Squeezing through my toes

Crystal blue waves
Pushing salt water to shore

Energetic kids
Building sandcastles

Sun so bright
Going through my sunglasses

Sunset going D
O
W
N

Sunset Beach
Joy Board, Grade 3
Buckner Elementary School, KY

Christmas Cookies

Stir and mix,
Mix and stir!
Make up the batter,
It's best when they're fatter!

Put them on the tray.
In the oven, then pray!
Sweet icing is the best!
After this you will need a rest!

Ally Ochs, Grade 1
St Vincent De Paul Elementary School, MO

Boats

Boats skimming through
the water
Orca style
Jumping up and down
the coast
Scaring fish
out of their wits
Leaving ripples
in their place

Francis MacEachron "Mac" Boggs, Grade 3
Hunter GT Magnet Elementary School, NC

Red

Red is a beautiful color because it is so bright.
It stands out just like a star in the night.
Red reminds me of Christmas times,
Shopping, and standing in long lines.
It also reminds me of Christmas cheer,
Because I love the song Rudolph the Red-Nosed Reindeer.

Jasmyn Johnson, Grade 3
Evangel Christian Academy, AL

Birds

B eaks
I n their nests all the time
R eady for their babies
D ignified
S plendid at flying

TJ Kaminsky, Grade 2
Ponte Vedra Palm Valley Elementary School, FL

The Frog
The frog jumping in the deep shallow water
the lily pads swaying like the clouds in the sky
the frog diving like a fish
the frog eats its seaweed
green slimy seaweed
the frog jumps over the rough rock
wet frog ribits out of the shallow water
and ribits away
the frog

Isha Chauhan, Grade 2
Buckner Elementary School, KY

Christmas
Presents
Holiday
Santa
Chimney
Stockings
Candy
God's Son

Christmas

Mason Ebert, Grade 2
Ponte Vedra Palm Valley Elementary School, FL

Mother
M ommy is kind and lovely.
O ur time together is special.
T hings may go bad but she is always there for me.
H er hugs and kisses are wonderful.
E ven when I am scared she's there.
R eally I love her and she loves me.

Sean Celestin, Grade 2
James E Sampson Memorial Adventist School, FL

I'm Thankful
At home, I'm thankful for my dog, my cat and my mom.
At school, I'm thankful for the Bible, my friends and my teachers.
At meals, I'm thankful for Cheez-Its, water and chicken and dumplings.
In nature, I'm thankful for animals, trees and fish.
I'm thankful to God because He made everything.

Veronica Johnson, Grade 1
Guardian Angels Catholic School, FL

My Family

My family lives in Tennessee.
There are 6 of us.
We share toys and books.
We do agree.
And still we are a family.

Our hair is black.
Are eyes are black.
Our skin is brown, too.
We're all that we can be;
That's why I love my family.

We laugh and play,
We work and share,
We see each other every day.
The world's a good place to be;
Because, we are a family.

Jaylen Bussey, Grade 1
Byrns L Darden Elementary School, TN

Cats

Cats.
Big,
Small,
Short,
Tall,
Cats.
Furry,
Fluffy,
Smooth,
Sleek,
Cats.
House,
Farm,
Wild,
Stray,
Cats.

Erica Lim, Grade 3
Columbia Catholic School, MO

Butterfly

Fly butterfly
Fly to the sun
See the flowers then go
Fly home

Mackenzie Chabot, Grade 1
Oakland Primary School, SC

Butterfly

Fly butterfly!
Fly to the zoo.
See the animals.
Then fly home.

Aleighah Allen, Grade 1
Oakland Primary School, SC

Fly Butterfly

Fly butterfly
Fly to my house.
See the house.
Then fly home.

Jaidyn Holland, Grade 1
Oakland Primary School, SC

Frog

I have a frog.
I had a toad.
It went under the log.
Then it went in the road.

Adam Gasper, Grade 1
New York Elementary School, MO

Animals

Eagles are white
Polar bears are too.
I love all animals,
And they love you.

Mckinley Farese, Kindergarten
Evangelical Christian School, TN

Christmas Is Really Fun
Christmas day is here,
I run down the stairs!
I open up my presents,
Santa Claus really cares.
We roast marshmallows by the fire,
Christmas is really fun!
We like to sing Christmas songs,
Santa brings joy to everyone.
Austin Engelhardt, Grade 1
Westlake Christian School, FL

I Make a Christmas Wish List
Christmas is my favorite holiday,
You get toys under the Christmas tree.
The tree is big with a star on top,
It is very cool to see.
I make a Christmas wish list,
I hang my stocking by the fireplace.
I leave out cookies and milk,
Santa goes down the chimney space.
Dean Bakkalapulo, Grade 1
Westlake Christian School, FL

Teachers, Teachers Everywhere
Teacher, teachers everywhere,
Teacher, teachers have no hair.

Teacher, teachers are so funny,
Teacher, teachers hop like bunnies.

Teacher, teachers are so cool,
Teacher, teachers ROCK the school!
Abbey Kellerman-Baker, Grade 2
Spoede Elementary School, MO

Football
Amarrius is my name
Football is my game
I love to throw the ball
And even when I fall
Football is my sport
Amarrius Prince, Grade 1
Oakland Primary School, SC

Cloud
The big, puffy cloud
In the big blue sky
Flies like a bird
In the sky.

The gray, smooth cloud
Is a dolphin jumping
Up in the Atlantic Ocean.
Gabrielle Valantiejus, Grade 3
Wellington School, FL

Jesus Is with Everyone
Jesus was born on Christmas,
He is God's Son.
People came to see him,
Jesus is with everyone.
I play my Christmas CD,
"Jingle Bells" is my favorite song.
I like "Rudolph the Red Nosed Reindeer,"
I wish Christmas would be very long.
Demetri Hackett, Grade 1
Westlake Christian School, FL

We Have a Snowball Fight
Christmas is super fun,
We have a snowball fight.
We hide behind our dads,
We go outside in the night.
I throw a snowball at my cousin,
And then we make a fort out of snow.
My sister hit me with a snowball,
Now it's my turn to throw.
Tomas Huy, Grade 1
Westlake Christian School, FL

I Like the Lake So Much
I like to go swimming
I like to play in the sand
We also go camping
We see movies
I like to go fishing
Alyson Palumbo, Grade 1
Oakland Primary School, SC

Butterfly
B utterflies are nice. Butterflies
U se pollen
T o
T urn into food.
E veryone likes them.
R unning away
F rom predators
L ucky little guys
Y ay! I like butterflies

Michael Bledsoe, Grade 2
Robert E Lee Expressive Arts Elementary School, MO

Writing
A learning adventure to me would be,
to write about cool things, sometimes at school.
Haunted houses and carnivals.
Writing is what I like the most,
in my mind I can go coast to coast.
I write every day and everywhere,
I have some ideas to share.
This is an adventure to me
because I can go anywhere I want to be.

Nevaeh Crow, Grade 3
Washington Lands Elementary School, WV

The Howling Wind
The wind is a Howler Monkey
Elegantly leaping from tree to tree
Howling whenever frightened or threatened
Squealing while hanging onto a vine
Reaching for the high tree tops of Banyan trees
The wind is a Howler Monkey

Rohini Sharma, Grade 3
Hunter GT Magnet Elementary School, NC

Changing of Leaves
Fall is a beautiful time because
leaves began to change so many colors.
They turn red, orange, and yellow.
When you are crossing a river
you can see so many different kinds of trees.

Jamarree Frierson, Grade 1
Oakland Primary School, SC

The Dream
I like the grass and butterfly clouds.
When I hum, all the animals come to me,
the blue sky turns to rainbows
and the birds sing and dance.
I clap my hands and grass and trees
turn into cotton candy,
and lakes turn into seas.
I have fields of flowers
and an island where I am a mermaid
and a queen in my dream.
Jelise Jones, Grade 2
Lee A Tolbert Community Academy, MO

Keyboard
Type type type.
You can type words on a computer.
Click clack.
A red line is on the screen.
It means you spell words wrong.
Type type type.
Click clack.
A green line is on the screen.
Click the right mouse button hit ignore.
Type type type.
Kyra Isaacson, Grade 3
Camden Station Elementary School, KY

Snow
Snow is cold.
Snow is wet.
Snow does not make you sweat.
Snow is cool like a pool.
Snow does not make you late.
Just go on in the gate.
I've never seen snow before.
If I did, I would not ignore...
Going outside to play,
On a cold snowy day.
Paige Colston, Grade 3
Many Elementary School, LA

The Wind
Do you hear the wind in the night —
Just to howl like an owl?
The invisible wind —
Swooping and soaring —
Howling whining.
While you are lying in your bed.
The wind howls night and day.
Sydney Kuczenski, Grade 3
Love Memorial Elementary School, NC

Watermelon
Watermelon, watermelon
I love watermelon
Red watermelon
Yellow watermelon
Watermelon, watermelon
So juicy and sweet.
Olivia Parker, Grade 1
Cool Spring Elementary School, NC

Autumn
A ll gather up to eat turkey
U se kind words to family
T ake care of family
U nbelievable ham
M ake apple pie
N o more food, I'm full!
Johanna Urso, Grade 3
Central Park Elementary School, FL

Ice
Ice, ice
I love ice
It can go in water,
Ice is so crunchy,
It feels so good in my throat,
I love ice.
Dalton Jones, Grade 1
Cool Spring Elementary School, NC

A Wonderful Winter

I think winter is very fun,
and I think it's season number one.
People playing all the day,
winter is so very great, hooray!

Snow is dancing in the sky,
Like frozen icicles, me, oh, my.
Chunks of snow on the ground,
friends and family all around.

Making a snowball and snowman,
make him look like Jackie Chan.
Give him a scarf, mittens, and a jacket,
even give him a fancy tennis racket.

Before this snow day ends,
I'll show my mom all my new friends.
I'll say with a big grin "Good-bye."
"It was a great snow day," I said with a sigh.

Linh-Dang Bui, Grade 3
Nesbit Elementary School, GA

Full Moon

Quietly sitting, looking up
Brightly shining looking down.
We both listen, to the night sounds.
Peacefully, like we are statues.
Waiting to see what happens next…
In life.
He smiles at me. I smile back.
Then he gracefully fades away.
And it is morning…already.
And it goes on like this for quite some time…
Until he is just a sliver in the quiet dark night sky.
Then he comes back.
    Full.
He glows the most beautiful glow.
Like he is the sun.
And he is so far away so far away, that he looks like a big dented balloon up in the sky.
With stars by his side.

Jessica Donoho, Grade 3
Camden Station Elementary School, KY

My Dog, Lucy
L ovable friend,
U nbelievable dog.
C ute pup.
Y oung pet!
Maggie Ward, Grade 1
Evangelical Christian School, TN

Dogs
D ogs are lots
O f trouble
G reat for a pet
S ometimes they are bad.
Sam Holland, Grade 1
Evangelical Christian School, TN

Fall
F all
A pples
L eaves
L ove it.
Becca Ikle, Grade 1
Evangelical Christian School, TN

Funeral
Waiting to pass him.
I never thought I loved him this much.
I can feel the blueness in my eyes.
I refuse to remember him.
Jacob Trimble, Grade 3
Camden Station Elementary School, KY

Witch
The witch is trying.
She is learning to flying.
She hit a tree with her broom.
Now she is in the tomb!
Brittany Watts, Grade 3
Doyle Elementary School, LA

You Are Having a Picnic I See
I can see you under a tree,
with your picnic basket in your hand.

You are having a picnic I see,
you are having a picnic under that tree.
May I have a grape or three?
Kathryn Wheatley, Grade 2
Alpena Elementary School, AR

Butterflies
I like butterflies
They are cute and come in all colors.
I like to run after and play with them.
Butterflies like flowers.
They fly high in the sky.
That's why I love butterflies.
Sierra Furman, Grade 1
Oakland Primary School, SC

Christmas Comes
Who is that in the sky?
Flying in a high point of the moonlight
It is Santa flying high
He has a huge bag of toys
Plus reindeer flying with their paws
And of course no claws
Zachary Humphrey, Grade 3
Alpena Elementary School, AR

Little Froggy
Little froggy with no color,
I look at your friend and he is duller.
You swim across your favorite stream
To be in the sun and let it beam.
When you get hungry you eat a shrimp,
Don't eat too many or you'll be a blimp.
Cooper Thomason, Grade 3
Hillsdale Christian School, OK

Weekend Fun

Weekends are the time for fun.
You can have more fun
in the weekend sun.

If I was going to the lake,
I would take lots of cake.

A good attitude I want to keep
so on weekends I still will need lots of sleep.

Burgers on a roasted bun,
oh, my favorite
Yum-yum-yum!

So come on over to my house to play
and we will have a great, fun day.

Don't you agree that
weekends are not
the time for
getting stung
by a bee?

Ashley Allen, Grade 2
Westminster Christian Academy, GA

Slithery Snake

Slither, slither.
The snake slithers along.
Slither, slither
The snake slithers on.

BOOM, BANG, BOOM, BANG!
The mean hunter is here.
BOOM, BANG, BOOM, BANG!
The snake got shot.
BOOM, BANG, BOOM, BANG!
The snake sneaks silently sideways into the spooky, scary, slimy rain forest.

Stomp, Stomp!
The mean hunter is furious.
"I'll get you someday!" screams the furious hunter.

Collin Deshler, Grade 3
Camden Station Elementary School, KY

Jesus Loves the Children
Jesus is a Holy Spirit,
He was born in the hay.
Jesus loves the children,
I love Christmas day!
Santa Claus brings me presents,
He puts them under my Christmas tree.
My cousins come to my full house,
They sleep on my bed and stay with me.
Chaylee Wenn, Grade 1
Westlake Christian School, FL

Cloud
The white, puffy cloud
In the clear blue sky
Runs like a chubby hamster
In her pink ball.

The baby, striped cloud
Is a kitten
Playing in its fluffy bed with her yarn.
Cassidy Ingram, Grade 3
Wellington School, FL

December
D eer prancing
E xciting time of year
C elebrate
E xtremely fun
M ary
B ells
E verybody decorates
R eindeer
Emily Grace Beaudry, Grade 2
Macon-East Montgomery Academy, AL

Noodle Fish
Seven noodles in a dish
Swim around like skinny fish
I make them swim and swirl and swish.
With my teeth, I grind and squish.
All my little noodle fish.
Dennis V. DeHart, Grade 1
Oakland Primary School, SC

His Sleigh Is Jingly and Red
I open a present on Christmas Eve,
Before I go to bed.
I think about flying with Santa Claus,
His sleigh is jingly and red.
It would be cool to fly with Santa,
I would wait on the roof with the reindeer.
I would play 'I Spy' with them,
Until Santa was near.
Eleanor Gruber, Grade 1
Westlake Christian School, FL

When Santa Claus Comes to Town
When Santa Claus comes to town,
He leaves presents for everyone.
I love to see my brother open presents,
It is wonderful and fun.
My brother tackles me to show he's happy,
He is grateful for having me.
I love to open my presents,
Santa leaves them under the tree.
Grace Weaver, Grade 1
Westlake Christian School, FL

Santa Brings Us Presents
Jesus was born in Bethlehem,
He was born on Christmas day.
Santa brings us presents,
We open them and play.
We go out and eat on Christmas,
We see our family.
I love to play with my brothers,
They are happy to play with me.
Elijah Bakkalapulo, Grade 1
Westlake Christian School, FL

Tae Kwon Do
I do tae kwon do.
I learn to kick.
I am a white belt.
I wear a uniform.
I will try my hardest.
Dominic Brown, Grade 1
Oakland Primary School, SC

Time Creeps

In the night,
The time creeps slowly
but surely.
As the baby cries,
The time creeps on
As the moon shines.

Jaydon Richardson, Grade 3
Alpena Elementary School, AR

Santa

Santa come here, Santa goes there,
He gives me a teddy bear.
I have to go to bed at night,
While he is on his long flight.
He is fast,
He never comes in last.

Gabe Robbins, Grade 2
Macon-East Montgomery Academy, AL

Roses Are Red

Roses are red violets are blue
I'm a cheerleader
How about you?
I have my shirt,
my skirt, my pom poms,
and my team too.

Kiera Brown, Grade 1
Oakland Primary School, SC

My Dog

I have a dog.
He likes to play.
He plays so much,
He may play all day.
He is black.
His name is Bogey.

Ann Marie Csucsai, Grade 1
Cool Spring Elementary School, NC

I Am Grateful

I am grateful for the smell of peaches
and the feel of a sunny day.
I like the taste of a good hot dog
and the look of my style.
I like the feel of my dog
and the sound of quietness.

Zach Rhodes, Grade 2
Lee A Tolbert Community Academy, MO

Just Like My Daddy

Daddy I know you are not here
because you are saving the world.
Don't be sad I'll be a good girl.
I'll make A-B you will see
because when I grow up
I want to be just like you Daddy.

Kalysta Figaro, Grade 1
Oakland Primary School, SC

My Dad

My dad is in the Air Force.
He works on jets.
He gives me a big hug
and a big kiss when he gets home.
I love my dad so much.
He is my hero.

Anissa Rogish, Grade 1
Oakland Primary School, SC

Football

Football, football such a great game.
Football, football it's not lame.
Football, football so much fun.
Football, football you have to run.
Football, football make a touchdown.
Football, football kick it out of town.

Logan Hine, Grade 3
Columbia Catholic School, MO

My Little Brother

My little brother is a pain.
He kicks me in the knee,
He looks like a little sweetheart to my mom
But definitely not to me
He tried to use my lipstick but that's not going to happen
My little brother is only 2
But he has all my clothes inside his room.
If my mom takes him anywhere
He'll start to pull people's hair.
I tell them that we're sorry
But then they start to stare,
When I'm playing with my American Girl
He grabs her and grabs me.
He'll put his face close to mine,
And loudly start to scream.
I told him not to do that
But he never, ever stops.
The next day my mom caught him
Taking more and more of my stuff,
Oh, my little annoying brother.

Serina Schoenlank, Grade 3
Virginia A Boone Highland Oaks Elementary School, FL

Johnny Appleseed

I am Johnny Appleseed. My real name is Johnny Chapman.
I wonder why I wear this pan on my head.
I hear birds singing.
I see many places to plant my apple seeds.
I am Johnny Appleseed.
I pretend that I am magic.
I feel good about planting seeds for everyone.
I touch the warm ground.
I worry that my seeds will not grow.
I cry because I can't stay and watch them grow.
I am Johnny Appleseed.
I understand that it is important for me to plant the seeds
I believe that someday there will be lots of apples.
I dream about walking as far as I can planting seeds.
I try to plant as many as I can.
I hope they all will get sunshine and rain to grow.
I am Johnny Appleseed.

Hunter Midcap, Grade 1
Mineral Wells Elementary School, WV

Gone

Crying
Why did she have to go?
Wishing I could see her just one more time.

Shedding tears
Like a dog sheds its fur
Wishing I could see her just one more time.

I loved her with all my heart.
Why did she have to go?
Wishing I could see her just one more time.

Kicking, screaming,
Yelling I NEED HER, I NEED HER!
Wishing I could see her just one more time.

Leaving me.
Wishing I could see her just one more time.

GONE

Andrea Stolworthy, Grade 3
Buckner Elementary School, KY

Woods

Tall grass
Tall trees
Weeping willow like a crying tree.
Thorn bushes.

Bird's chirping in the trees,
Wind blows, a cool breeze.

Leaves rustling,
Water rushing,
Rough bark,
Sharp thorns.

I look out my window and I see nature.
I smell the flowers in the woods.
Fresh air
Woods, a good place where nature roams around.

Chad Cooper, Grade 3
Camden Station Elementary School, KY

I Love You Sun

Sun, sun
I want you back
  when the moon is out.

Sun, sun
Can you see
  you belong with me.

Sun, sun
You are back in the morning
  and I love you.

Kristie Nance, Grade 2
Alpena Elementary School, AR

Six Flags

People loudly yelling
The roller coasters zoom
Quick like lightning.
Lots of people.
And enormous roller coasters.
Getting icy cold soda
Right for a sizzling hot day.
Seeing lots of fun rides
Saying in my mind
I don't
Want to leave.

Omar Calixtro, Grade 3
Buckner Elementary School, KY

Hunting

Hunting can be very fun,
Unless you accidentally forget your gun.
If a deer comes out,
You better not shout.
When you go home early,
A deer might pop out,
So you better load your gun,
That's when it starts getting fun.
The best part about it is getting to eat...
THE MEAT.
That's hunting.

Nick Slaydon, Grade 3
Many Elementary School, LA

Fun Fall

Fall is as fun
as a bouncy ball.
In fall leaves turn
red, yellow, purple, orange.
Fall is fun!
I don't want fall to be done.
Did I mention brown?
Let's make a fall crown.
The wind is blowing.
The stars are glowing.
I love fall!

Shelby Ehly, Grade 3
Eagle's View Academy, FL

Me and My Grammy!

Me and my Grammy,
Watching TV,
Glancing at the screen
Going outside,
Feeding ducks
With bread
Seeing brown and green ducks,
Looking for bumpy golf balls.
Glancing in the water,
Seeing our reflection.
Me and my Grammy!

Kara Zarotny, Grade 2
Buckner Elementary School, KY

Christmas Star

The Christmas star...
Shiny
Bright
Sparkly
Glittery

Five pointed tips
Smaller than a sheet of paper
An ornament on the tippy-top of the tree
So high in a tree
You can almost touch it.

Katelyn McMath, Grade 3
Landmark Christian School, GA

Michael
Michael is kind and playful.
Michael loves to fish and to play soccer and hunting.
Michael thinks what makes him a good friend is kind and playful
Michael's nickname is Chukie.

Hayden McLemore, Grade 3
Briarwood Christian School, AL

Trees
Trees are very cool.
The branches are very still
I love trees so much.

Hailey Blinderman, Grade 2
Virginia A Boone Highland Oaks Elementary School, FL

Iguanas
Iguanas are green.
Iguanas are so pretty.
I like iguanas.

Randi Argow, Grade 2
Virginia A Boone Highland Oaks Elementary School, FL

Six Flags
The Mindbender is green, the Ninja is red.
They are curvy and fast and you may bump your head.
I want to come and visit again and ride the rides in the wind.

Erin Rice, Grade 2
Bramlett Elementary School, GA

Iguanas
Iguanas are cool.
They shake a lot in the pool.
I love iguanas.

Omer Erez, Grade 2
Virginia A Boone Highland Oaks Elementary School, FL

Waterfalls
Waterfalls are cool.
They are very beautiful.
Waterfalls are pools.

Libby Levy, Grade 2
Virginia A Boone Highland Oaks Elementary School, FL

Back in Time

Once when I went back in time,
I found the world's first dime.
I played with cavemen and dinosaurs,
I saw saber tooth tigers and heard their roars.
I helped Albert Einstein develop $E=MC^2$,
I built Amelia Earhart's plane and say "fly if you dare."
I helped World War I soldiers fight in the war,
I did all that stuff and much, much more.
Incredibly happy describes how I feel,
Boy this "Periods of Time" book makes everything feel so real!

Jordan Singer, Grade 3
Virginia A Boone Highland Oaks Elementary School, FL

4th of July

Fireworks scream eeeeep eeeeeep.
Fire crackers crack crack crack.
Bursting with color like a rainbow.
Dims down to the ground.
And when it went up
it was like it was joining the stars above
then falling falling falling.
Down to the ground
as another one went up a flower bursting open
as we sit on the back porch.

Julie Jakabiak, Grade 2
Buckner Elementary School, KY

November

I can't believe November is already here.
After all, it's the eleventh month of the year.
The leaves on the trees are already turning.
We rake them in piles, ready for burning.
The squirrels are busy gathering nuts for winter.
Getting ready for much colder weather.
Soon the trees will be bare.
We will begin to feel the chill in the air.
Thanksgiving is coming upon us fast.
Don't forget to have a big, big blast!

Tanner Heafner, Grade 3
Norris Childers Elementary School, NC

Fall Is Here!
Fall is here,
It's time for fun.
The leaves are changing,
Autumn has begun.

It's time for laughter…
Time for joy.
Halloween's a holiday
You can't ignore.
Children are busy trick-or-treating.
Parents, get ready for some candy eating.

Cool breezes are blowing
October is a blast.
Change your clocks back an hour,
'Cause Thanksgiving is coming fast.
Hannah Prince, Grade 3
Caneview Elementary School, LA

Bells
I hear a tiny sound
The bell is round.
It is silver and shiny
The bell is so tiny
I have it on a string
What joy will it bring?
Dawson Strickland, Grade 2
Macon-East Montgomery Academy, AL

Blue Dragon
I have a pet.
His name is Blue Dragon.
He brings me luck.
When he sees ice cream,
he screams and blows blue fire.
I fly on him at night.
He is purple with blue eyes,
a long tail, sharp teeth, and paws
and eats anything.
I met him in my backyard
and I hide him in my laboratory.
Isaiah Jones, Grade 3
Lee A Tolbert Community Academy, MO

My Star
Glowing and glittering
In the night
The light so bright

Special
Kind
The leader of all

Courageous, bounteous, loving
Caring, bountiful, fidelity
Loyal, flittery, shiny

Credence, spruce, odorless
Fresh, clean, superb
Agreeable, holy, beautiful
Paige Aronhalt, Grade 3
Landmark Christian School, GA

Peace, Love, and Happiness
My Papa lightens up my heart
He's like an angel up above
He makes me feel ten feet tall
Like a whale in the soothing ocean
I knew he loved me from the start

You make my heart feel like gold
You make me feel like a pot of gold
At the end of the rainbow

I knew that you were thankful for me
From the day I was born
Because you are always doing
Nice things for me
I love you with all my heart
Diondus Williams, Grade 3
A H Watwood Elementary School, AL

A Horse
A horse eats off a bark,
A horse eats leaves,
A horse eats an apple.
Julie Lee, Grade 3
Cool Spring Elementary School, NC

Raindrop

A raindrop is wet.
A raindrop makes a splash.
A raindrop makes a puddle.
The raindrop's color is my favorite color — BLUE.
A raindrop makes me think of a shower.
Raindrops make me think of sweatiness.

Justin Ortiguera, Grade 2
Ponte Vedra Palm Valley Elementary School, FL

A Game of Baseball

Hitting,
Catching,
Batting,
Running,
and...
Fielding.

Drew Wright, Grade 2
Ponte Vedra Palm Valley Elementary School, FL

Autumn

A ll the leaves are crackling when they fall
U se whipped cream on the pie
T he turkey could have gravy
U se a lot of gravy on mashed potatoes — it's good
M y turkey is good
N o more pie!

Gabrielle Ray, Grade 3
Central Park Elementary School, FL

Smiles

I smile loving when I get loved by my mom and grandma.
I smile shy when I meet new people.
I smile toothy when I feel excited.
God smiles at me when I smile at Jesus.

Allison White, Grade 1
Guardian Angels Catholic School, FL

Fishing

Catching, Casting
Boating, Rowing
And Reeling.

Stewart D. Slayden, Grade 2
Ponte Vedra Palm Valley Elementary School, FL

Autumn

I can see autumn.
I can see me celebrating my birthday.
I can see kids jumping in leaves
I can see my dog jumping in leaves.

I can smell autumn.
I can smell fresh blueberry pie.
I can smell cinnamon brooms.
I smell my mom still making her coffee.

I can hear autumn.
I can hear leaves falling.
I can hear leaves crackling under feet.
I can hear my dog barking and kids laughing.

I can taste autumn.
I can taste fresh sweet potato chips.
I can taste my mom's pumpkin muffins.
I can taste fresh maple syrup.

I don't need to look at a calendar to know it's autumn.

Kira Diehl, Grade 3
The Parke House Academy, FL

Trouble

I've got two brothers.
How 'bout you?
Jack is four and George is two.

Sometimes we fight
And sometimes we play.
We like to sword fight night and day.

We jumped on the beds,
But Mommy told us not to.
We hit our heads and my eye turned blue.

We got in big trouble.
We all went to "TIME OUT"
That's what you get when you jump all about.

Will Dougherty, Kindergarten
Evangelical Christian School, TN

Merry Christmas!
I taste:
The mint candy canes
The fresh ham
The corn upon my taste buds

I see:
The Christmas feast and all of the yummy food
The people crying with joy of the birth of Jesus

I smell:
The fresh ham from the oven
The mints delicious mints
The huge feast on the table

I hear:
The birds chirping joyful songs while the sun rises
The sound of the jingle bells and the beautiful Christmas carols

I feel:
The snow just touching my fingers
The juice from the berries
The warmth of the fire on my back

I know:
That Christmas is amazing

Ella Hayes, Grade 3
Riverhill School, AL

Spooky House
Ghost Ghosty
Lightning frightening
Spooky scary
Wooden floors,
"Creak"
Doors creeping open…
Slam shut,
Ghosts whisper in the dark corners,
Ghosts run up and down stairs
Looking for someone to give nightmares to…
Boo!
Sorry, did I scare you?

Hailee Bates, Grade 3
Camden Station Elementary School, KY

Autumn

Autumn leaf, autumn leaf
Up high in the tree.
I climb up to get it.
It's too late, it falls beneath my hands.
It floats down the stream.
I remember its beauty as it floats away.
Just like I'll remember the beauty of autumn.

Winter is like a blanket.
It helps autumn go to sleep.
As the seasons come and go,
Autumn is one of the most beautiful of all.

Eve Parent, Grade 1
White Sand School, FL

The Beginning

Leaves start out as a bud,
Waiting for the summer sun.
Growing beautiful and full,
With the promise of more to come.
When the wind grows cooler,
They start to change colors.
It gives us a view of God's
Beautiful wonders.
After the change, they crash to the earth —
Feeling free from the tree.
Then they become crunchy and brown,
Praying to be once more in the summer sun.

Nataleaha Gutierrez Mora, Grade 3
Love Memorial Elementary School, NC

I'm Talking School!

I'm talking school!
I'm talking Pledge of Allegiance to the flag!
I'm talking numbers, letters, words!
I'm talking pencil, paper, computers, Smart Board!
I'm talking writing journal, science journal, social studies journal, math journal,
      morning work journal!
I'm talking car line, lunch line, snack line, line up at the door to go outside!
I'm talking reading, science, social studies, math, art, Spanish, religion, P.E.!
I'm talking school!

Michael Gomes, Grade 1
Blessed Sacrament School, FL

Raging River

As I hear the river gurgle over little pebbles
And see it raging down its path through the woods,
I forget all my worries.
The sun shines on my back and my feet in the cool water.
It always brings peace over my body.
As I sit and enjoy the peaceful moment,
I realize it's getting late.
The sun is sinking fast.

Heather Snow, Grade 3
Columbia Catholic School, MO

God's Creation

God is love.
He made everything.
He made trees so green and birds that sing.
He made everything.
He made air so we may breathe
and fish that swim in the deep blue sea.
He even made me.
God is love.

Susanna Reid, Grade 2
Evangelical Christian School, TN

I Am Grateful

I am grateful for my hands
because they help me pick up tables and chairs.
They help me eat macaroni that smells cheesy.
They help me open doors
for people in wheel chairs.
They help me write paragraphs
about my family, and iron clothes
for my brother and cousin.

Martice Steward, Grade 2
Lee A Tolbert Community Academy, MO

The Farm

I wish I lived on a farm.
I love to play with the animals in the barn.
The cat slaps at a piece of yarn.
The pigs are in the barn.
I love my day at the farm.

Kayla Allen, Grade 1
Oakland Primary School, SC

My Brother

My brother is the best.
Only he makes a big mess.
We like to play games,
And play with my cousin James.
Josh my brother and I like cake,
Only it is hard to make.
My grandma sends stuff on my birthday.
I told her she doesn't need to pay the money I want today.
I wish we were home schooled.
Then play in the pool.
I think it was a good day.
Even though I didn't get paid.
No matter where I sleep
I will look through a peephole and see my brother asleep.

Brandon Burke, Grade 3
Alpena Elementary School, AR

Hummingbirds

Hummingbirds flying in the graceful wind
as fast as a shark swimming in the water
fast
    faster
        even faster
flying the wind
swoop
    swoop
Flying as calmly as a flower sitting in the grass
approaching to the flowers.
hummingbirds wings falling asleep
quickly hummingbirds flying back home
quickly quietly.

Luke Parish, Grade 2
Buckner Elementary School, KY

Snow

It looks like white rice.
It sounds like "crunch, crunch, crunch."
It feels like white, hard, wet rock.
It tastes like ice and water.
It smells like wet winter.
I love snow!

Alexandra Peek, Grade 2
Ponte Vedra Palm Valley Elementary School, FL

My Computer Artist
My pumpkin
Is a Computer Artist.
He likes to print stuff,
From the computer.
Print, Print, Print!
He likes to play
A lot of games.
It is so sad
He will soon rot!
William Gangler, Grade 3
Coral Springs Elementary School, FL

Burning Up
I see ashes in the air
I am looking for the fire
I see a building burning up
I see a person
OH NO
The firemen don't see him
"Firemen"
The firemen got him
He is safe
Elijah Skaggs, Grade 2
Buckner Elementary School, KY

All About Me
Jack
Athletic, strong
Jogging, pitching, running
Kind to his friends
Brooky
Jack Dicen, Grade 3
Briarwood Christian School, AL

Autumn
A wesome pie
U ltimate turkey
T ree leaves falling
U nsoft leaves
M ake me thankful
N oses are very cold
Skylar Miedema, Grade 3
Central Park Elementary School, FL

Puppy Presents
I hope I get a puppy for Christmas,
I'd really like it a lot.
It would be so soft and cuddly,
"I can't wait!" I thought.
I will dress my puppy up in a Santa hat,
I will take him outside in the snow.
We will play for hours and hours,
And then I will drink a cup of hot cocoa.
Nicholas Diaz, Grade 1
Westlake Christian School, FL

Cloud
The shapely, white cloud
In the blue, windy sky
Swims like a dolphin
In the clear water.

The big, brown cloud
Is a horse
Galloping in the round pen.
Joshua Buchan, Grade 3
Wellington School, FL

Cloud
The dark, fluffy cloud
In the beautiful sunset sky
Ran like a black cat
In the moonlight.

The tiny, spotted cloud
Is a ladybug
Crawling on the blue, small flower.
Brielle Cash, Grade 3
Wellington School, FL

Fat Cat
My cat is fat.
He sits in my lap.
His name is Willy.
He waddles when he walks.
But, he is my fat cat.
Adriana Hicks, Grade 1
Oakland Primary School, SC

Autumn Comes Again

I can see autumn
I can see big black cats chasing mice.
I can see colorful leaves falling from trees.
I can see harmful bats flying creepily.

I can smell autumn.
I can smell delicious pumpkin pie coming out of the oven.
I can smell spices like cinnamon.
I can smell soup with carrots in it.

I can hear autumn.
I can hear wind whistling through trees.
I can hear leaves crackling when people step on them.
I can hear mice squeaking when cats chase them.

I can taste autumn.
I can taste a warm crispy turkey.
I can taste puffy yellow corn.
I can taste cookies melting in my mouth.

I don't need to look at the calendar to know it's autumn.

Anna Voicu, Grade 3
The Parke House Academy, FL

Christmas

Tomorrow is Christmas and this is what I want
All my presents will come from my aunt
I will get a ball, a scooter, and a belt
Beware, get me something I don't want and you'll melt

We'll put up the tree
And we will say tee-hee
All the presents will be for me
And I'll smile with glee

When I went to sleep I heard a bump
Out jumped Santa with a thump
I said Oh-my oh-my
He'll be ok he's a jolly old guy

Derrian Brown, Grade 3
Nesbit Elementary School, GA

Thanksgiving

Thanksgiving comes once a year.
Family and friends are all here.

We play and eat, how much fun
to get together with everyone!

Turkey and stuffing how very yum
We can't wait to have some!

Jared Weingard, Grade 3
Virginia A Boone Highland Oaks Elementary School, FL

The Amazing Earth

The amazing earth, the fiery sun
The warm breezes on a summer's day
The amazing earth, deep blue sea
The northern blue ice caps melting, melting
The amazing earth, the trees, plants that makes us live
The amazing earth, Mother Nature, the hurricanes, tornadoes, and floods
The amazing earth gives life and takes it away
The amazing earth, the cycle of life.

Skylar Rasmussen, Grade 3
Tropical Elementary School, FL

I'm Talking Catholic School!

I'm talking Catholic school!
I'm talking principal, teachers, students!
I'm talking religion, Wednesday Mass, praying before lunch!
I'm talking math, science, social studies, reading, P.E.!
I'm talking pencils, erasers, highlighters, computers, maps, globes!
I'm talking words, spelling, vocabulary, numbers, addition, subtraction, writing,
    poems, stories!
I'm talking Catholic school!

Nicholas McClure, Grade 1
Blessed Sacrament School, FL

Friends

They are nice and caring.
They talk to me.
They make me feel good.

Friends

Abby Bennett, Grade 2
Ponte Vedra Palm Valley Elementary School, FL

Forest
Forest animals
Animals like nature's air
Animals like you.
Bhrajit Thakur, Grade 2
The Parke House Academy, FL

Animals
Animals are cool
Animals are cool nature
You pet animals.
Cole Hinson, Grade 2
The Parke House Academy, FL

Sharks
Sharks are cool and swim
Sharks swim with their pointy fins
Sharks live in the sea.
Neal Thompson, Grade 2
The Parke House Academy, FL

Nature
Flowers and trees blow
Singing sweet birds in their homes
Birds are so pretty.
Peyton Depasquale, Grade 2
The Parke House Academy, FL

Jaguar
I am a jaguar
I live in the rain forest
I love my home here!
Tulsi Patel, Grade 2
The Parke House Academy, FL

Nature, Nature, Nature
Nature is roses
Roses make nature pretty
Roses are pretty.
Kennedy Kircher, Grade 2
The Parke House Academy, FL

Dolphins
Dolphins o dolphins
So soft, you are my inspiration
Created by God!
Allison Bernt, Grade 3
Columbia Catholic School, MO

Bald Eagle
It is a cool bird
It is very sensitive
It is the state bird.
Luke Barrett, Grade 2
The Parke House Academy, FL

Spider
I am a spider
I love the rain forest here
I live in a web.
Camryn Halley, Grade 2
The Parke House Academy, FL

Nature
Birds fly over trees
Wow, what a sight look at that
The Earth is the best!
Beau Bichler, Grade 2
The Parke House Academy, FL

The Boston Freeze
My skin has goose bumps
I left my big coat outside
Hot chocolate…mmm.
Daniel Tressler, Grade 2
The Parke House Academy, FL

Rain Forest of Time
I like rain forests
Jaguars climb tall trees a lot
I like great spiders.
David Manning, Grade 2
The Parke House Academy, FL

My Little Princess

My little princess is quite odd!
Instead of wanting a castle,
She wants an iPod.
She has a split personality:
One's mean, one's bratty.
When she wants something,
You better not say "No,"
Or else she's just going to BLOW!
So now you know my little princess is definitely spoiled,
So just make sure she doesn't get boiled!

Aniaya Murray-Smith, Grade 3
Coral Springs Elementary School, FL

Frosty Where's Your Hat?

Winter time is lots of fun.
I put on my boots and begin to run.
The excitement of the night before brings lots of snow and joy for all.
All the children in the town hope that Frosty comes around!
I look to my left and to my right.
As Frosty appears from out of sight!
We placed the hat on top of his head.
Do you think we should call him Ted?
The snow slows down and we all know it's time for Frosty to go.
We do not cry a single tear for he will be back next year.

James Daniel Fitzpatrick, Grade 3
Norris S Childers School, NC

Dad's Work

Two billowing towers
Like soldiers guarding the sky
Restaurant music going through my ears and out
Gourmet food heading inside me
Tastes like little pieces of fun to tingle my tongue
Fresh air going in each nostril, smooth slick pole
Rugged red carpet going over
Down over down jumpy as a kangaroo
Heart beating normally hands sitting as still as a statue
Finally we head home once again

Khalid Asad, Grade 3
Buckner Elementary School, KY

Alyssa

Fun as flying in the sky
We are reaching friends
Fun!
Reaching each other
our arms go round and round
each other
fun!
our arms reaching each other's necks
hugging each other so tight
we'll explode on each other
f
u
n
friends forever
BFF
Best friends forever!
Alyssa my best friend forever
At the end we reach each other
together we're on our way to see each other
forever
We'll see each other till the end of our life.

Grace Marylee Baker, Grade 2
Buckner Elementary School, KY

Jorge Batievsky

J ewish
O rganized
R unner
G enius
E xtreme

B rilliant
A thletic
T alented
I ndependent
E xcellent
V aliant
S mart
K ind
Y oung

Jorge Batievsky, Grade 3
Virginia A Boone Highland Oaks Elementary School, FL

The Great Football Run
Okay…guys
There are five seconds left till half time
So let's try to score okay
Let's do uuuh!

Forty-seven quarterback keep
On one ready, "Break!"
When I come out of the huddle
I hear the shouting and screaming of the crowd

Down set-hut
As I see the QB get the ball
I block a defender
Me and some other guys
Get great blocks
As we block
I smell the hot smelling hot dogs

And the QB is gone in a flash
He's to the —
Fifty the forty
The thirty
The safety is catching up
And he is tackled at the twenty "eeeerr!"

Jared Mercer, Grade 3
Camden Station Elementary School, KY

What Will I Be When I Grow Up?
What will I be when I grow up?

Will I be a police officer?
I would…help people stay safe.

Will I be a firefighter?
I would…put out fires, save people from fires.

Will I be a worker for my dad (Select Veneer)?
I would…sell wood and buy wood.

Will I be a teacher?
I would…teach kinds, and help people learn.

Reid Kilibarda, Grade 3
Camden Station Elementary School, KY

I Am From

I am from apples
I am from board games
    like Yahtzee and card games
I am from hobbies
    like cooking, teaching and shopping
I am from friends
    Jan, Mindy, Emily
I am from riding my bike
    and playing with my brother.

Jaylyn Gray, Grade 3
Alvaton Elementary School, KY

Mr. Frog

Once there was a little frog
Sitting near on a log
Under a green tree
All alone.

Mr. Frog saw a bug
Crawling by.
Out came his tongue
And the bug waved good-bye!

Eric Henderson, Grade 3
Carver Elementary School, NC

The King Lion

I wish that I was a lion
because it is a protective animal,
strong and king of all the land.
The cheetahs and I will run in circles,
slide down a water slide,
and eat spaghetti and hot dogs.
There will be a moon walk
where we can all jump and dance
until we can't jump and dance anymore.

Kendale Gillum II, Grade 2
Lee A Tolbert Community Academy, MO

Shelf Elf

S hare crackers with them.
H ere and there.
E lves are watching you.
L iving in your house.
F or you and for me.

E verywhere.
L aughing.
F or you on December 17th

Trent Watson, Grade 2
Macon-East Montgomery Academy, AL

Lions and Tigers

The lions and tigers can run together.
They sleep by day and hunt by night.
They are both meat eaters.
They both use their fur as camouflage.
They both use their tongues to clean.

Michael Dillon, Grade 1
Oakland Primary School, SC

I Like Horses

I like to ride horses.
Horses are pretty.
Horses like to run.
Horses like to jump.
I love horses.

Makayla Rockholt, Grade 1
Oakland Primary School, SC

Basketball

Hi, my name is Ethan.
And I like to play basketball.
It is really easy.
I am unique and no one is like me.
I am good at basketball.
Do you want to go against me?

Ethan Perkins, Grade 1
Evangelical Christian School, TN

Autumn

A n awesome day
U ncooked turkey — put it back in
T he turkey is tender — time to eat
U nlikely weather — it is still too hot
M arvelous day
N ot turkey again!

Ashley Kochman, Grade 3
Central Park Elementary School, FL

Thanksgiving

T hanksgiving is a time for family
H elping make dinner and set the table
A special day for spending time together
N o schoolwork to worry about
K itchen filled with lots of food
S haring delicious dinner
G athering around the table
I nviting friends and family
V ery special time
I love spending time with my family
N ow it's time for dessert
G reat food and a very full belly

Zachary Foster, Grade 3
Virginia A Boone Highland Oaks Elementary School, FL

Me

Thomas
Active, physical, determined
Son of Bryan and Suzette
Who loves reading, writing, and learning
Who needs love, animals, and my bike
Who feels happy, sad, and mad
Who gives a hand, smiles, and money
Who fears ghosts, means dogs, and mean teachers
Who would like to see Africa, New York, and Europe
Who dreams of flipping, riding on a unicycle, and swimming again
Who lives in the country
Bacon

Thomas Bacon, Grade 2
Robert E Lee Expressive Arts Elementary School, MO

Bunnies

Bunnies cute and fun you play with them
All day long they jump in the woods
Playing with other bunnies
You feed them a carrot they nibble on it I hear
The crunching sound they eat the carrots
When night comes they get in their bed and go to sleep
Cute and fluffy

Bunnies

Savannah Gordon, Grade 3
Buckner Elementary School, KY

Christmas
I love the snow
I love the shows
I love the lights
I love that there are no fights.

Saniyah Ashah, Grade 3
James E Sampson Memorial Adventist School, FL

Smiles
I smile lovingly when people do nice things for me.
I smile cute when I get dressed up.
I smile tired when I get in from gym.
God smiles at me when I do nice things for people.

Anna Montesanti, Grade 1
Guardian Angels Catholic School, FL

Watch
Tick…Tick…ugh please, please
Turn it off I do not like the noise please, please turn it off!
Noise, noise too much noise. Please, please turn it off it's
very annoying noise, noise, noise everywhere.

Lily Francis, Grade 3
Camden Station Elementary School, KY

Flowers
These flowers are perfect in every way,
I started to pick them at the beginning of the day.
But when my mommy makes me come in,
she makes me put the flowers in a bin.

Caroline Bowen, Grade 2
Evangelical Christian School, TN

Catfish
He is a pet. He is as strong as a football player.
He is sparkly like a diamond.
Also he is sparkly silver.
He is so strong that he can lift another fish.

Cole Evans, Grade 3
Camden Station Elementary School, KY

Fall

The leaves will fall
All day long.
The breeze
Will blow the leaves
Down to the ground.
When leaves fall down,
They are found.
The trees stand tall
All of fall.
Let's go home.
It's been a long day.
That's enough fall
For today.

Faith Herrera, Grade 2
Eagle's View Academy, FL

Fall Is Coming Soon

I can tell fall is coming soon.
The leaves on the tree in the backyard,
Are turning colors.
Now that it is fall,
I can see different colored leaves,
Everywhere I go.

I can tell fall is coming soon.
People are getting their rakes out.
People are busy.
Animals are preparing for winter.

Fall is coming soon.

Chance Silvers, Grade 3
St Paul's Lutheran School, OK

Football

All slippery and wet on my hand
Getting ready to throw the ball
I say blue 42 hut-hut-hike

Drop back in the pocket
Avoiding the pesky defenders

Finally throwing the ball
Getting hit hard in the turf
Watching the touchdown
I'm getting up slowly
Heading towards the sidelines
Football

Sam Pate, Grade 3
Camden Station Elementary School, KY

Good-bye Training Wheels

Worried
Feet on peddles
Shaky
Go
Go
Go
Grass, houses, fences, and trees fly by
Tires bump
Cool wind blows
Go
Go
Go
Happy, fast, and fun

Connor Tierce, Grade 1
Round Lake Elementary School, FL

Ice Cream

Ice cream, ice cream
I love ice cream
Strawberry
Chocolate
Banana
Vanilla
So yummy and so good.

Victoria King, Grade 1
Cool Spring Elementary School, NC

Magical

M y wish comes true on Christmas
A n angel is my Christmas wish
G ena is the new angel on Christmas
I t's a jolly Christmas
C alling angels from above
A ngels watch over us
L ove comes from all around

Emily Brooks, Grade 2
Macon-East Montgomery Academy, AL

Winter

Winter's snow is like a blanket of clouds
lying on the ground.
It is as blank as an empty page
that hasn't gotten used yet.
At night time if you look through your window
you will find frost on your windowsill.
Winter is as gorgeous as a twinkling star at night.
Winter is as cold as an icicle that is crystal clear.
Winter is as black and white as a picture that was taken years ago.
Winter is when you're trapped inside because it is too cold to go out to play.
Winter is one of the most wonderful seasons of all.

Catherine Crabb, Grade 3
Lynn Fanning Elementary School, AL

Spots of Black and White

In the fields I see shades of black and white,
I hear the sounds of long, low beautiful sounds
I see it eating grass

I sit on my porch watching it circle around the barn,
I'm distracted by the crow of the roosters,
The oink of the pig,
The meow of the cat, the click of the crickets swimming in hay
And...

I'll never stop staring

Olivia Asher, Grade 3
Buckner Elementary School, KY

Halloween

A creepy black cat,
A devil chasing after a bat
A big ghostly ghoul, screeching such a big howl,
A witch in a cemetery ditch,
A zombie helping an employee.
A moan coming from a haunted home.
Oh such a scary night,
Such a ghostly sight!
It's time for bed,
Let's hope we don't drop dead!
Happy Halloween!

Meira Kowalski, Grade 2
Wellington School, FL

The Night
Snow drifts down slow and silent,
The evening sky kisses my face,
But suddenly…

The crisp air turns into shadows of darkness,
Stars brighten up the sky,
Owls hover over the snow,

The night,
The full moon, like a snowball,
The smell of cookies fill the air,
The hot cocoa, like lava,

A special night,
Bells ring like the jingle in the cold crisp air,
The song of stars,
A choir of angels,
Street lights flicker on,
A Christmas night.

Chloe Arvin, Grade 3
Camden Station Elementary School, KY

Grass
The grass is green as a leaf,
The grass waves in the wind,
The grass is speaking to me saying don't cut me,
I say we have to because you're getting long,

The grass feels smooth like a stone,
The grass smells like a mushroom,
The taste is a meatball spaghetti worm sandwich,
I hear whistling from the wind flowing across the grass,

The grass is like a calm waterfall,

Grass sitting until we mow the lawn,
Right there in the hot sun in the same spot,
I call its name,
It calls back to me,

Grass, Grass, Grass…

Luke Payne, Grade 2
Buckner Elementary School, KY

Axel
Leaping through the air,
Sliding across glistening ice,
Spinning in the air —
An ice skater,
Flying free.
Snowflakes fall gracefully,
Mimicking my every move.
Fading light,
Another hour,
Tired,
Soaring, skating,
Muscles tense,
Bounding into the air,
Spinning like a blur,
Landing gracefully,
One of the snowflakes,
Sliding down the hill,
Excited,
The center of the storm of a million snowflakes.

Laurel Seibert, Grade 3
Hunter GT Magnet Elementary School, NC

My New Baby Brother
I am at home with family and friends
Waiting for my new baby brother
They said he would be my best friend
The door opens wide, I hear oohs and aaahs!
I see the new baby
It made a noise!
Everyone is gathered around it
Hey it's a boy!!!
I am bigger but no one sees me
Everyone is looking at the new boy
I do some somersaults
I yell, "Look! It's a parade outside!"
But no one even looked at me
Everyone said "Shhhh! Come and see your brother!!!"
I sneak closer to get a peak
Brown hair and blue eyes
Oh my gosh, just like me
It's my baby brother!!!!!!!!!!!!!!

John R. Schmid, Grade 3
Hunter GT Magnet Elementary School, NC

Bats

Bats are sleeping all day long.
Bats are singing all night long.
Bats have fun all the time.
They sleep in the coal mine.
You can hear their wings whooshing through the air.
Watch them, watch them if you dare.
They fly like crazy all through the night.
Some are frightening, some are a sight.
Bats have fangs that are super freaky,
But I am not scared of them even if they are creepy.

Brett Welch, Grade 3
Norris Childers Elementary School, NC

I Wish

I wish I could be a chocolate horse
and I could eat myself up,
or be a butterfly so I could flutter all around.
If ice cream came from the sky,
it would fall on me and I would be cold.
When I went to school
I would smell like vanilla or strawberry.
If meatballs fell from rainbows and
french fries were clouds,
I would fly up there for dinner.

Jeanelle Brown, Grade 2
Lee A Tolbert Community Academy, MO

Halloween Scares

Black bats chasing me,
An owl hooting a song in a ghostly tree,
A monster oozing slime,
Eight hairy pumpkins scaring kids away,
Witches stirring brew and bloody zombies lay,
Trick-or-treating kids,
A freaky mummy opens a coffin lid,
Now it's time for a scary dream,
Have a good dream about a bloodstream!
Happy Halloween!

Ashley Jones, Grade 2
Wellington School, FL

I'm Talking Gymnastics!

I'm talking gymnastics!
I'm talking front flips, back flips!
I'm talking team names, team coaches, team spirit!
I'm talking floor exercises, balance beams, bars, vaults!
I'm talking leotards, bare feet, tape grips, chalk on the bars, music on the floor!
I'm talking judges, points, scores, cheers, posters, 1st place, 2nd place, 3rd place,
    trophies!
I'm talking gymnastics!

Kendall Laplante, Grade 1
Blessed Sacrament School, FL

A Tree

I want to draw a tree
because it takes the sun away from me.
A big and green tree, and full of leaves.
It has a huge tree house
where I put all my things.
I feel like I want to stay in my tree
protected under his shadow
because the sun is burning me.

Gabino Serrano, Grade 3
Virginia A Boone Highland Oaks Elementary School, FL

I Am a Softball Hero

I am up to bat
I swing at the ball
I hear a big splat
I run to first and I burst
Then I run to second and have a second with the coaches
I run to third and see a herd of people
I run home
Yippee, I got a home run!

Mary Caroline Campbell, Grade 2
Briarwood Christian School, AL

Sweet Chicken

My mommy asked me what I wanted for dinner.
My answer was sweet chicken.
I love sweet chicken because
It is a sweet taste with sugar, and butter.
It is yummy in my tummy.

Kianna Mike, Grade 1
Oakland Primary School, SC

Football

F antastic
O vertime
O ut of bounds
T ouchdown
B all
A thletic
L eague
L ength of field

Noah Schwartz, Grade 3
Virginia A Boone Highland Oaks Elementary School, FL

Lost My Stuff

I couldn't find my homework
I couldn't find my school
I couldn't find my teachers
And that was against the rules!
I can't find my crayons
I can't find my markers
I can't find my pencils
So there is no use in going without proper utensils

Madison Skylar Fives, Grade 3
Virginia A Boone Highland Oaks Elementary School, FL

Imagine a Day…

Imagine a day…
of a snowball war with your best friend.
You both get hit with snowballs at the same time
and your faces were cold.
Then you go sledding for two hours.
Imagine you go in for steaming hot cocoa.
Imagine a day of fun.

Luis Pelayo, Grade 3
Robert E Lee Expressive Arts Elementary School, MO

Bugs

Oh bugs, those slimy squirmy worms that dig in the dirt and eat the dirt,
And those beetles, how disgusting are their clicking and clocking,
And those spiders with 8 legs,
Man, those creep me out,
But those crickets that hop in the grass,
The clicking and clocking and clicking and clocking drives me nuts.

Ethan Saunders, Grade 2
Evangelical Christian School, TN

I Like…

I like to dance.
I like to prance.
My dog's name is Skeeter, he is a boy.
I play with him like a toy.
I like to play computer.
I like to ride my scooter.
I like my new boots.
I heard a flute.

Sydney Hall, Grade 1
Evangelical Christian School, TN

Fashion Fairy

Fashion Fairy, Fashion Fairy
So high in the sky,
Where are you going to
So high, so high?
Turning into a mermaid
And jumping in the sea!
Fashion Fairy, Fashion Fairy
Can't you take me?

Blannie Baum, Grade 2
Richmond Elementary School, OK

Raindrop

Raindrop raindrop falling from the sky
flip and flop there is a drop.
Raindrop raindrop falling from the sky
look there's more. Watch it pour.
Raindrop raindrop oh how you fall
the whole town gathers to watch you all.
Raindrop raindrop falling from the sky
the whole town leaves and says good-bye.

Julia Hamilton, Grade 3
Columbia Catholic School, MO

Matthew

Matthew is my baby brother.
He likes to play with me.
Matthew is very funny.
He likes to feed the puppies.
I love Matthew.

Laura Pollock, Grade 1
Oakland Primary School, SC

Christmas Time

Santa Claus gives us presents,
Santa Claus is nice.
He likes the cookies I give him,
He likes the ones with spice.
Christmas is a special holiday,
That's when Jesus was born.
The shepherds followed the star,
And the angels blew a horn.

Alex Franco, Grade 1
Westlake Christian School, FL

Jesus Is a Special Man

I can't wait until Jesus' birthday,
He was born on a starry night.
Mary and Joseph went to a manger,
After they followed a bright light.
I will pray to Jesus in my room,
Because of all he's done for me.
I love him very much,
I want the whole world to see.

Jensyn Nixon, Grade 1
Westlake Christian School, FL

Getting a Christmas Tree

We pick out a Christmas tree,
We look for a tall one.
They put it on our rooftop,
I think that's so much fun.
We decorate the tree at home,
We put a star on the tippy top.
A train goes around the tree,
We push it and then it stops.

Ava McEwan, Grade 1
Westlake Christian School, FL

What Makes Me Happy

When I am with my dog
I am happy
When I am with my mom and dad
I am happy
And try to never be sad.

Trevor Myers, Grade 1
Oakland Primary School, SC

I Love New York
My name is John, I like New York.
It's a fun place to visit, and take a walk.
There's lots of fun things to be found,
In Little Italy there's the DeSalvo playground.
If after playing I get hungry,
It's time to get pizza from Lombardi's.
We always stay in the middle of the city
But I like to visit the Statue of Liberty.
I like to visit the M&M store,
And go to the Empire State Building,
But most of all I love to go to Toys R Us
And ride the ferris wheel.
The subway is fast, but not once inside,
Turtle taxis are great to just take a ride.
The best thing about New York is the Museum of Natural History.
The Phantom of the Opera is my favorite play,
But Mary Poppins had great things to say.
I've seen the Easter parade, the hats were all handmade,
But what I really want to see,
Is the Macy's Thanksgiving Day Parade.

John DiMaggio, Grade 1
St Ann Elementary School, LA

Alaska
Oh, how I love Alaska!
In Alaska, it rains enough to get you wet.
The climate is a soggy one.

Oh, how I love Alaska!
I love the smell of the ocean.
It gives you a sense of the land.

Oh, how I love Alaska!
In the ocean, I saw a starfish.
It was six points in an orange glow.

Oh, how I love Alaska!
My family's vacation was a beautiful trip.
We saw so much, we learned so much, and we want to go again.

Oh, how I love Alaska!

Alison Collums, Grade 3
St Paul's Lutheran School, OK

Autumn Comes

I can see autumn.
I can see leaves blowing in the wind.
I can see reds, browns, yellows, and orange leaves soaring in the sky.
I can see people knocking on the door.

I can smell autumn.
I can smell a mountain of marvelous mash potatoes.
I can smell terrific turkey.
I can smell scrumptious stuffing.

I can hear autumn.
I can hear leaves crackling.
I can hear laughs and enjoyment filling the room.
I can hear people saying Happy Halloween!

I can taste autumn.
I can taste delightful corn.
I can taste sweet sensational desserts.
I can taste outstanding gravy in my mouth.

I don't need a calendar to know that it's autumn.

Aiza Zubair Saeed, Grade 3
The Parke House Academy, FL

Where I'm From

I'm from my cat
I'm from my lovely friends
I'm from the sky
I'm from a blooming rose,
I'm from my sisters
I'm from my brothers
I'm from a tall mountain
I'm from my mom and dad
I'm from my pretty creek
I'm from my dog
I'm from an apple falling down from a tree
I'm from school
I'm from a grape picked off a tree
I'm from eating a banana up
I'm almost from everywhere

Miracle Miller, Grade 2
Buckner Elementary School, KY

Halloween/Christmas
Halloween
dark, scary
playing, trick-or-treating, driving
house, candy, holiday, hot chocolate
playing, opening, working
snowy, cold
Christmas
Hannah Nepple, Grade 3
Lakeland Elementary School, MO

The Dog and Cat
A dog and a cat,
Once played catch.
But the cat got hurt, and said,
"Let's play baseball with a bat,"
"Okay," said the dog to the cat.
They played till they dropped,
and laughed all day long.
Helena Guenther, Grade 3
Northridge Christian School, OK

Fall
Down, down, down
The leaves fall down
They twist and they turn
They go crunch, crunch, crunch
Onto the ground and...
Then they shatter into little pieces...
Of dust
Meredith Popeck, Grade 2
Buckner Elementary School, KY

The Sun and the Moon
The grass is green,
The sky is blue.
The sun is happy,
And so are you.
The sun is bigger than the moon.
The moon is sleeping at night,
And the world is too!
Penelope Sugg, Grade 2
Bramlett Elementary School, GA

Stars
The bright yellow stars
are in the black sky at night
shining at me.
Narayana McGill, Grade 2
Roseland Park Elementary School, MS

Butterfly
A pink butterfly
is flying in the blue sky
dancing in the wind.
Veronica Lord, Grade 2
Roseland Park Elementary School, MS

Max the Fish
Max, the lazy fish
in the rectangular fish tank
sleeping his life away.
Deniya Freeman, Grade 2
Roseland Park Elementary School, MS

The Deer
A brown thirsty deer
searching in the dark forest
finding some water.
Bryce Lott, Grade 2
Roseland Park Elementary School, MS

Water Snake
A long water snake
in the breezy Hawaii
sleeping in an old boat.
Kelton Seal, Grade 2
Roseland Park Elementary School, MS

The Bluebirds
The chirping bluebirds
in the nest of an oak tree
practicing how to fly.
Cade Thorman, Grade 2
Roseland Park Elementary School, MS

The Missing Tooth

Call the doctor quickly, this is what I feared,
This is really serious, my sister's sweet tooth disappeared!

When she craves a snack,
She eats pickles by the pack.

She asks for broccoli, cauliflower and peas,
Candy and ice cream make her sneeze.

When I have a sugar rush,
All my candy she will crush.

She doesn't want cake or a chocolate kick,
She is begging for a carrot stick.

Halloween is really boring,
While we eat candy, she is snoring!

Call her weird, call her a bore,
But she's the healthiest girl, I'm sure!

Shoshana Sklar, Grade 3
Virginia A Boone Highland Oaks Elementary School, FL

A Day at the Circus

One day I went to the circus to watch a great show.
I am glad I live in South Florida, at least it does not snow!

Even in this hot weather the clowns caught a cold.
Their noses were red and puffy, and their heads were really bold.

The children ate their cotton candy, boy oh boy, they were all so sticky.
And when the elephants came out, the tent smelled really icky.

The horses came out galloping, and one of them sneezed.
What a funny moment, until a man fell off the trapeze!

At the end of the show, came one of the best parts.
The tigers jumped hoops, while monkeys drove go-carts.

The crowd clapped and cheered, the kids left with prizes and balloons.
Everybody had a wonderful time on this grand Sunday afternoon.

Jonathan Baran, Grade 3
Virginia A Boone Highland Oaks Elementary School, FL

Blazing Beach

Cold icy water
Bursting in my arms

Coconuts falling
Like lightning

The sun
Shines like a million stars

Waves curving
Like the breeze

Popsicles melting
Like tears in your eyes

Kids playing
With sandcastles

Volleyballs
Volleying back and forth
Brian Dill, Grade 2
Buckner Elementary School, KY

Horses

Run fast my little horses
As fast as fast as you can go
Close your little eye my little horse
And dream about your mommy
Cool wind blowing on your face
In the night sky
In the morning
Run fast
My little horses
In the race
Do not lose
My little horses
Because you can go so fast
In the moonlight
You won the race
Big trophy in your hands
Smiling
Leah Rankin, Grade 2
Buckner Elementary School, KY

Fall

Leaves falling from the trees
Crunching as they hit the ground
Red, yellow, orange leaves
Hitting the ground like snow

Cool breeze rushing against my face
Big piles of leaves calling my name

Pumpkins being carved
On Halloween night

Stars shining between the leaves
Staring back at me
Fall
Anna Carden, Grade 3
Buckner Elementary School, KY

Water Flows

Water flows
Water flows
Down the river it goes.
Water flows
Water flows
Right between my toes.

In my pool the water flows all over me.
Splish n splash in the bath
Fun and functional for me
Water is money,
Water is Earth
Please don't waste it
We need water to live.
Jessica Wechsler, Grade 3
Country Hills Elementary School, FL

Space

S tars all around
P laces, like Earth, are in it
A ll around are planets
C ats would float about
E arth has life but none of the others do!!
Alana Starr, Grade 3
Banyan Creek Elementary School, FL

Me
India
Creative, funny, helpful
Daughter of Nicole and Thad
Who loves my Mom, my Dad, and my pets
Who needs love, humor, and my family
Who feels sad, weird, and fun
Who gives hugs, presents, and animals
Who fears Chucky, evil ghosts, and Morgan
Who would like to see my Grandma and Grandpa
Who dreams of Chucky, evil ghosts, and being a lifeguard
Who lives in Columbia, Missouri
Johnston

India Johnston, Grade 2
Robert E Lee Expressive Arts Elementary School, MO

Finn, Finn!
Finn, Finn!

He's a fish that swims around
Sometimes up, other times down.

Finn, Finn, he looks like a clown
Sometimes it looks like he's wearing a gown.

Sometimes he's hard to be found
When he is swimming around.

Finn, Finn!

Carlos Puyo, Grade 2
Spoede Elementary School, MO

Christmas Tree
A Christmas tree
is good for putting colorful presents under,
It has colorful ornaments on it,
It can be big or small.

Though it is pokey and has different shapes of ornaments,
It makes me feel delighted.
It doesn't move and it doesn't make a sound;
It usually has presents under it.

Coulter Maginnis, Grade 3
Landmark Christian School, GA

Autumn

My dad and I look at the amazing, colorful trees.
My sister and I walk in the beautiful, crackling, leaves.
My mom and I make a tasty cornbread.
The big, orange pumpkin was slimy as I was carving it,
My family was eating a yummy, cinnamon bread!

Ava Lovelady, Grade 2
Wellington School, FL

Sophia

Sophia
loving and nice
watching sports, hunting and playing sports
loyal, good, kind, gentle
Soph

Ross Godbehere, Grade 3
Briarwood Christian School, AL

A Snake

I wish I had a snake,
I could bring it to school.
It would have black and white stripes on it,
It would be a great pet for me,
It would be a corn snake.

John Martin, Grade 2
Cool Spring Elementary School, NC

Dolphins

Dolphins jumping in the graceful sky like the mermaid does
Lives in the blue smiling ocean
As the sun rises in the ocean
I can see you in the clear blue sea
Dolphins dancing in the dancing blue ocean

Aubrey Moye, Grade 2
Buckner Elementary School, KY

Squid

Squid
Pink, deadly
Inks, sticks to rocks, gets disturbed by ships
It is horrifying.
Cephalopod

Jonah Lanning, Grade 3
Clinton Christian Academy, MO

Yummy
I like spaghetti
because it is delicious.
I like it with lots of cheese.
I love the sauce.
Adreanna Burkes, Grade 1
Oakland Primary School, SC

I Like Rainy Days
Rainy days are fun,
I like to run in the puddles,
I like to play in the puddles,
Do you like to play in the puddles?
Jericho Oliver, Grade 1
Oakland Primary School, SC

Life
Flowers bloom
People sing
I am smart
You are too
CiCi Yang, Grade 3
Kerr Elementary School, OK

All About Me
Christopher
Loving, funny,
camping, playing sports,
telling others about Jesus.
Christopher Workman, Grade 3
Briarwood Christian School, AL

Riley's Blog
active, funny
football, soccer, swimming
very nice to others
RiRi
Wesley Kathryn Shaver, Grade 3
Briarwood Christian School, AL

All About J. J. Jetplane
Nice, medium
Swimming, football, basketball
Nice to other people
J. J. Jetplane
Julia Salem, Grade 3
Briarwood Christian School, AL

My Family
My mom is small,
My dad is tall,
My brother is nine,
I'm glad he's mine!
Natalie Harmon, Grade 2
Briarwood Christian School, AL

John Mathen
Kind, happy
football, baseball, powerful
always kind to others
Jam Jam
John Mathen Wierengo, Grade 3
Briarwood Christian School, AL

Lindsey
cheerful, intelligent
basketball, softball, swimming
kind to my friends
LG
Lindsey Lovvorn, Grade 3
Briarwood Christian School, AL

Riley Traves
Nice, loving
tennis, basketball, swimming
loves cheerleading a lot
sunshine
Ward Combs, Grade 3
Briarwood Christian School, AL

Puppy Paws
Dashing through the rain
My mom shakes the umbrella
As water plops to the ground

BARK! BARK!

I immediately ran to the cage
The dogs were so adorable

The manager stepped in she slowly opened the cage

He jumped into my arms
Squeak! Squeak! Squeak!

I tickle his little puppy paws
His black paws tickle my face

He licks my face
And smells my soft golden brown hair

My dog Mason and his little puppy paws!
Alaina Scott, Grade 3
Buckner Elementary School, KY

The Wild Ride
Screaming as me and Mom shake with fear
going up and down
up and down.

Screaming like you got kidnapped
as it jerks me
I feel like I'm going to explode
because of all the fear inside me.

Wind fighting against my face
like a twister
At the end we wish we could go again.

The wild ride
Stephanie Toth, Grade 3
Camden Station Elementary School, KY

Me Sick
Lonely on the couch
Resting quiet as a mouse
Going to get a cold drink of water
Cold like an iceberg
Nobody to play with because everybody is at school
Water rushing through the fridge
Telling myself there's nothing to do
I turn on the flashing TV
It woke me up
Drinking of my polar water
I change the channel
I turn the TV off
And went to the cold shivery basement
Playing rocking video games
Till 2:24
I lay back on the couch
Resting
Waiting for my brother and
Sister to get home

Nick Ward Prohaska, Grade 2
Buckner Elementary School, KY

I Am From
I am from Wendy's chicken sandwiches
I am from Dad's spaghetti
I am from Mom's Tuna Casserole
I am from the card game Uno
I am from the card game Phase Ten
I am from the board game Checkers
I am from making pretty jewelry
I am from doing 3-D puzzles
I am from swimming in deep water
I am from my best friend Kaylie
I am from my friend Trinity
I am from my friend Jillian
I am from Beach Bend Park
I am from Holiday World on the Voyage
I am from Grandma and Granddaddy's house, riding the four-wheeler
I am from playing the Wii Fit
I am from Spore Creatures on the D.S.
I am from playing with Buddy, my Grandma and Grandpa's wiener dog

Meghan Smith, Grade 3
Alvaton Elementary School, KY

Halloween

Halloween is finally here.
I go outside,
I feel the fear,
I feel the wind rushing down
on me,
Oh, the beautiful leaves,
Running trying to catch up
with me,
People are jumping out,
Scaring me.
Oh, that fearful night,
I will never forget.

Chase Porter, Grade 3
Cool Spring Elementary School, NC

Bird

I would like to be a bird
and build a nest and fly.
I would dive like a swimmer
to find sharks and fish.
I could close my eyes in the sky,
wag my tail or whisper and giggle
at the same time.
I might sneak a cookie from the jar,
spin like an airplane, twirl, and dance
or sneeze and cough.
I might hide and spy on people,
if I were a bird.

Nevaeh Mattocks, Grade 2
Lee A Tolbert Community Academy, MO

Me and You

I love you
You make a bird fly in my heart.
You make the world a better place for me
You are a bright light of love
You are a shining star
You bring peace to my heart
You are as beautiful as a rose
You are a good person
That Jesus sent down to the Earth
When I am with you,
I feel like I'm in heaven
Me and You forever.

Trent Gardner, Grade 3
Childersburg Elementary School, AL

Grandparents

G od bless you
R eally kind
A wesome
N ice
D onut lover
P opcorn lover
A lways fun
R adiant
E lk lover
N ut lover
T ester
S harp

Gavin Luckett, Grade 3
Clinton Christian Academy, MO

Red

The shape of red
can be a folder, candy,
a roller coaster,
or the color of success.
Red can be medium,
large, or short,
a heart, roses, stop signs,
or a colored gingerbread man.
Red is the color of anger.

Michael Lee, Grade 3
Lee A Tolbert Community Academy, MO

I Am Light

I am the light
That shines throughout the day.
But when it rains,
My light goes away.
Thereafter, my powerful sunlight
Makes my beautiful rainbow.
I am the light
That lights up your face.
I am light.

Lindsay Hoffmeister, Grade 3
Sabal Point Elementary School, FL

Katy Bi
Katy Bi
Chinese and gentle
ballet, piano, and reading
gentle, kind
Bumblebee
Mac McNamee, Grade 3
Briarwood Christian School, AL

Cole Scordino
Cole Scordino
funny and smart
football, baseball, dodgeball
they think Cole's funny
Colishes
Jenna Flannery, Grade 3
Briarwood Christian School, AL

Me
Hollis
Happy, creative
Singing, dancing, drawing
Makes friends laugh hard
Hollister
Hollis Macoy, Grade 3
Briarwood Christian School, AL

Dreamer
Amber
Loving, kindness
Cheering, riding, hunting
Love to have fun
Pups
Amber Wooten, Grade 3
Briarwood Christian School, AL

Ross
Ross
Nice and funny
Plays sports, hunting, watch TV
Lets everyone play fair
Buddy
Sophia Adam, Grade 3
Briarwood Christian School, AL

All Football Today
Davis
Honest, brave
Biking, running, jumping
Friends who laugh often
Milk-man
Davis White, Grade 3
Briarwood Christian School, AL

All About Me!
Emahn
skilled, funny
soccer, dancing, eating
play sports with them
Emahon
Emahn Haririan, Grade 3
Briarwood Christian School, AL

Quiet Kid
Bennett
quiet, creative
fast, active, spider like
I like to share with others
Bug
Bennett Milton, Grade 3
Briarwood Christian School, AL

All About Me
Jenna
Funny, loving
Dancing, cheering, swimming
Loves to help others
Littlebit
Jenna Fuller, Grade 3
Briarwood Christian School, AL

Oli
Oli is a monkey.
Oli likes bananas.
Oli likes to swing from tree to tree.
Oli is our mascot for our class.
Oli likes people and he likes you too.
Ainsley Schultz, Grade 2
Briarwood Christian School, AL

Christmas Morning
I taste:
Sweet chocolate, mints, and snow
I love tea on Christmas morning

I see:
My mom, dad, sister, dog, and cat
I love them so very much
They are watching TV

I smell:
Chocolate and candy and other sweets
But most of all my Christmas tree

I hear:
The dogs are barking
The cats are meowing
The kids are laughing

I feel:
Happy and cold
I feel good to be with my family

I know:
My family loves me very much and they make me feel good
They are important to me

Margaret Jenkins, Grade 3
Riverhill School, AL

There's Nothing Better Than My Pet
There's nothing better than my pet.
She's cute and cuddly and I bet,
that when I leave for the day,
she misses me but that's ok.
Because she knows I always come home
and that she will never be alone.
She counts on me in every way,
cause she knows that I'm here to stay.
So everyone, I think, should have a pet
and I bet,
That you will be as happy as I
And that my friend is not a lie.

Megan Auerbach, Grade 3
Virginia A Boone Highland Oaks Elementary School, FL

Where I'm From
I am from strawberries they are big and juicy.
I am from pineapple nice and sweet.
I am from Wii I used it with a big remote.
I am from Nintendo I am an electronic.
I am from iPod I am very pretty.
I am from helping it is fun to help.
I am from softball it is awesome.
I am from a lot of nice friends.
I am from Taco Bell yum it's good.
I am from Chick-Fil-A go chicken I love it.
I am from Cuddly Bear I love her a lot.

Jillian Rimel, Grade 3
Alvaton Elementary School, KY

My Football Days
In the cool, crisp fall, I love to play football.
We have twenty-one players on our team, so we play lean and mean.
I am in-between, my number is fifteen.
Being very tall, it's easy for me to run the ball.
When our team is on the field, they form a big shield.
I run the 31-trap, with a quick snap.
When I get free, no one can catch me.
When it's fourth down, we need to make a touchdown.
We throw the ball not to hit the pole, we want a field goal!
After the game we get a sweet treat, we gather around to eat.
We look at the score, it keeps us coming back for more!

Colton Ledbetter, Grade 2
Briarwood Christian School, AL

Asia
Asia
Funny, nice, A food friend
Who loves Recess, art, and lunch
Who needs love, mom, and school
Who feels happy, sad, hurt, funny, and sleepy
Who gives hugs, kisses, and presents
Who fears clowns, bats, and bears
Who would like to see my sister, the world, friends, and good dreams
Who dreams of Chucky, vampires, and ghosts
Who lives in a two story house
Schafer

Asia Schafer, Grade 2
Robert E Lee Expressive Arts Elementary School, MO

Summer Days
Grass swaying in the air
Birds flying
People cheering
Summer
A
U
G
U
S
T
Days
Megan Janssen, Grade 2
Buckner Elementary School, KY

My Fish Bubbles
My fish bubbles is very cool.
He swims around in a little pool.
He's a little blue and red.
Among the rocks he makes his bed.
His tank is pink.
I bet he likes it
That's what I think
He swims around the very green plants.
He never wears any pants.
He also swims around the tank.
He cannot swim around the bank.
Rebecca P. Vercher, Grade 2
Briarwood Christian School, AL

Beautiful Fall
The fall time is a very special time.
It is a time of giving thanks.
I am thankful for so much.

The fall time is a very special time.
It is Thanksgiving time.
It is so pretty and the trees are changing.

The fall time is a very special time.
God paints new colors on our Earth.
This fall time is so very beautiful.
Zarah Douglas, Grade 3
St Paul's Lutheran School, OK

My Cousin's Birthday in Florida
Walking in sand
Sun setting over the horizon
Waves hitting against the shore
Listen
Splash, shells scattered
Covering soft wet sand.

Fresh air,
Warm breeze
A bright moonbeam
Shines down on me.
Stars light up the night sky.

Shadows glooming.
The smell of cake fills the air
Laughter.
The memories of me
Talking to my cousins come back.
My cousin's birthday in Florida.
Ben Williamson, Grade 3
Camden Station Elementary School, KY

Alexander Toms
I am a boy
I hear you
I see I can see
I wish I got the car washed
I feel happy when it is Sabbath
I hate to feel frustrated
I get angry when something happens
I am puzzled by not getting my work right
I dream about two dogs
I wonder why I can't get my work done
I plan to go to the state fair
I hope Monday we don't have school
I know something
I understand that people can talk
I learned something new
I value my family
I love all people
I am afraid of lightning
Alexander Toms, Grade 2
Berea Jr Academy, SC

My Friend

Where, where is my friend?
I can't find him anywhere.
I look in my backyard,
He is not there, but I will not give up.
I think I hear him.
Is he upstairs, is he outside, is he anywhere?
I'll find you!
He is under the bed.

Gabriel Breitenberg, Grade 2
Evangelical Christian School, TN

Swimming

You can swim and swim in a pool
The water makes you very cool

It's pretty and blue.
like a violet too.

The wavy water makes me
think of a jewel.

Alexandra Francisque, Grade 2
James E Sampson Memorial Adventist School, FL

Jesus Is God's Son

Jesus heals people when they need help,
Jesus is God's Son.
He was born on Christmas day,
He is so good to everyone.
I like Santa's magical sled,
He has a magical whip to make the reindeer go.
The reindeer fly to Florida,
Rudolph's nose has a red glow.

Chase Evans, Grade 1
Westlake Christian School, FL

All I Want for Christmas

When I went to see Santa and sat on his lap
I told him all I wanted was one new hat.
I could wear it in my dad's new truck.
Santa said he would try
I guess that's just my luck!

Connor Langston, Grade 1
St Vincent De Paul Elementary School, MO

Fish Tank

There once was a fish.
Who looked like a dish.
He lived in a tank.
In a great big bank.
Every day he had a big wish.

Shila Monae Weathers, Grade 2
James E Sampson Memorial Adventist School, FL

Memories

Memories are diamonds that are precious.
Memories are waiting to be kept to yourself.
Memories are something that I imagine.
Memories are photographs in my mind.
Memories are fiction and nonfiction.

Mark Oliver, Grade 2
Lee A Tolbert Community Academy, MO

Caleb

Caleb
hates school, likes video games
hitting hickory nuts, going outside, football
likes to play baseball
Smithy

Katie Payne, Grade 3
Briarwood Christian School, AL

Pepsi

When I drink it, it makes my taste buds dance inside my mouth.
When my tummy has Pepsi, it jumps around.
It pops around in the can when I drink the Pepsi,
The fizz goes up my nose, it stings so much.

Jeremy Cotton, Grade 3
Camden Station Elementary School, KY

Sun

Sun, oh, sun, you're so very bright,
Sun, oh, sun, you're a beauty even in the night.
Sun, oh, sun, you're a light to my eyes,
Sun, oh, sun, you're a beauty to sight.

Brandon Twenter, Grade 3
Good Shepherd Lutheran School, MO

Imagine

Monkeys bursting in beautiful purple.
A snake leading a colorful path of orange, blue, and brown.
There are so many shapes in a colorful piece of paper.
It pops with color and shape and size.
It is a balloon with bright, bright colors.
All of the colors are popping.
Imagine this.

John Diaz, Grade 3
Christ Church School, FL

Where I'm From*

Where I'm from is where birds sing a joyful song.
Where I'm from is where horses frolic in the meadows.
Where I'm from is a very happy place.
Where I'm from is where I hear kids screaming and having some fun.
Where I'm from is where streams go soothingly down to me.
Where I'm from is where I will be for a long time.

Megan Kaelin, Grade 3
Buckner Elementary School, KY
*Inspired by George Ella Lyons

I Want a World Where

Butterflies fly faster than bees.
Books are funny as clowns.
Sunflower plants are bigger than houses.

Ducks run as fast as lions.
Books cry with happiness when they are reading.
The wind kisses me.

Gerald Williams, Grade 3
Rivelon Elementary School, SC

A Rabbit in My Garden

Bouncing
Pouncing
Jumping
Thumping
Running
And going,
Hopping away.

Hannah Nagengast, Grade 2
Ponte Vedra Palm Valley Elementary School, FL

Thanksgiving
T urkey
H oliday
A wesome
N ice
K ind
S uperb
G reat
I nspiring
V acation
I ncredible
N ational
G lory

Ian Ostrowicz, Grade 3
Virginia A Boone Highland Oaks Elementary School, FL

Me
Wendy
Funny, happy, fun
Daughter of Cheryl and Terry
Who loves books, art, and cooking
Who needs love, fun, and humor
Who feels my body, cake, and mom
Who gives love and hugs
Who fears ghosts, some dogs, and cats
Who would like to see my baby brother, my cousin, and Texas
Who dreams of songs, zoo, and Jada
Who lives in a red house
Reams

Wendy Reams, Grade 2
Robert E Lee Expressive Arts Elementary School, MO

Your Two Families
Both nice families.
First your dad's.
Then your mom's.
But you love them both
Yes you do.
They love you with all of their heart and so do you.
I bet they would freeze in ice for you.
They love you so much yes they do.
They care about you too.

Connor Lewis, Grade 1
Riverhill School, AL

Christmas
Snow falling
Deer prancing
People calling
Everyone dancing

Singing songs
Wrapping presents
The Church bell gongs
Elves are pleasant
Lights twinkling
Everyone praying
Santa visits
Children playing

Logan Riggenbach, Grade 2
Washington Lands Elementary School, WV

The Forest on a Windy Day
Standing in the forest,
the wind blows like a flute,
whistling in my ears.
Dry leaves are blowing,
clip-clap, like tap shoes.
A flower petal is blown away,
but before it leaves your sight, it twirls around
just like a ballerina dancing.
A web is blown up, like a hot air balloon inflating.
The long grasses nearby are rippling, like a sea of grass.
Tree leaves tinkling and swaying,
then the wind stops.
The sun comes out and feels warm on my back.

Serena Pacella, Grade 3
Home School, WV

Ocean
Seagulls swooping
Down catching a mouthful of fish
The ocean sparkling like a diamond
Dolphins jumping out of the crispy white water
Puffer fish puffing up because of a fierce shark
Seaweed swaying in the ocean wind
The ocean is my paradise.

Austin Allen Reed, Grade 2
Buckner Elementary School, KY

Halloween, Halloween

I see a cat on the windowsill.
Creepy, ghostly mummies and a Frankenstein named Bill,
I see a spider crawling in a web.
The spider turned and said,
"Halloween, Halloween is an awesome scene!"
I see a cool pumpkin laying there.
It jumps up and gives me a scare!
I jumped up and laughed,
"What a scare!"

Sarah Ellmaker, Grade 2
Wellington School, FL

Blue

Blue is the ocean so bright.
Blue is blueberries so tasty and good.
Blue is my mood when I am sad.
Blue is the color of the sky so calm and slow.
Blue is the color of my blue jeans comfortable and cool.
Blue is my color
And it is mine
And no one knows
My color is blue

Hannah Tolbert, Grade 3
Evangel Christian Academy, AL

Raindrop

A raindrop is small
On a rainy day
But cannot grin
When people come out to play.
He tries to warn them
But it is too late.
Now when the kids come out to play again
All that is left are puddles.

Keegan Sobczak, Grade 2
Ponte Vedra Palm Valley Elementary School, FL

Trees

Trees are nice to watch
They are green to be healthy.
Keep trees nice to grow.

Peter Caillaux, Grade 2
Virginia A Boone Highland Oaks Elementary School, FL

Christmas

Christmas is a wonderful time of year.
There is family visiting family.
There is singing and cheering.
There is eating and playing.
There is talking and loving.
There are hugs and kisses.
There is wrapping everywhere.
Most of all, there is worshiping the Lord.
Christmas is a wonderful time of year!

Beau Ross, Grade 3
Many Elementary School, LA

Ice Cream

Ice Cream, Ice Cream
I love ice cream
Vanilla
Chocolate
Rainbow
Party, too
Ice Cream, Ice Cream
I love ice cream
So tasty and so good.

Jackson Swicegood, Grade 1
Cool Spring Elementary School, NC

Flowers

Red flowers, red flowers
Growing tall.
You smell so good
With blooms so tall!

Blue flowers, blue flowers
You are so blue
Looking so pretty
With your bright hue!

Aundra Foster Jr., Grade 3
Carver Elementary School, NC

Haunted Trail

There is fright
when you get in the
middle of the haunted trail.
You will feel crying and teary
steams.
You will feel the fright flowing
through your body,
when you come out
But you might not get out.

Lane Lester, Grade 3
Cool Spring Elementary School, NC

Football Team

Auburn
fearless, true
plays, runs, wins
War Eagle! War Eagle!
Tigers

Sarah Lowry, Grade 3
Briarwood Christian School, AL

All About Me

Lindsey
nice, beautiful
cheers, rides, eats
this is so fun!
cheerleader

Lindsey Best, Grade 3
Briarwood Christian School, AL

Autumn Leaves

Fall is beautiful.
Leaves gather
Changing colors from green
To yellow, red, orange, and brown.
People rake and bag them,
On October weekends.

Chelsea Peltier, Grade 3
Caneview Elementary School, LA

Exercise

I hear the pitter patter of feet, feet, feet.
But the smell of those feet is not sweet.
I don't like anything that is around me.
Even if they don't want to eat me.
I like to exercise.
But I don't like to fexercise.

Kristin Stewart, Grade 1
Evangelical Christian School, TN

Halloween Horror Night

A black cat creeping near me
Keeping its eye also on a tree.
As I trick-or-treat a ghostly ghoul walks up to me.
I watch in wonder of what I see!
Then a devil comes up to me
We go to an eerie place.
I hear screaming but I keep quiet.
Then a snake slithers right next to me.
Hundreds of zombies dining at dinner
Bats flying around a bloody dinner sounds disgusting!
But to witches, devils, and monsters it sounds delicious!
I tell the devil I have to go.
"O.K.", said the devil.
So I go home.
Say "bye, bye" little creepy bats.
So they flew away upon a mat!
Happy Halloween Night!
Oh, and you're all a creepy sight!

Sophie Bock, Grade 2
Wellington School, FL

All About Me

My name is Haleigh.
I have strawberry-blonde hair and green eyes.
My nose is soft and clean.
My skin is white and it feels smooth.
My ears are little and pierced.

I like to wear nice clothes.
Today, I am wearing a red and black shirt.
It feels soft and comfortable.
My Apple Bottoms pants are neat.
My tennis shoes are clean and soft.
My socks are new, but they smell stinky.

I, on the other hand, smell nice.
If you listen, my voice sounds clear and soft.
My favorite thing about myself is I am clean.
It is good that I am clean and not dirty.
Thanks for getting to know me.

Haleigh Tucker, Grade 2
Byrns L Darden Elementary School, TN

Imagine a Place...
Imagine a place...

where everything was candy
and trees were cinnamon
with rivers of chocolate,
lakes were Sprite,
grass were lines of mints and
the clouds are small pink
pieces of cotton candy.

Imagine!

Lashaylin Lewis, Grade 3
Robert E Lee Expressive Arts Elementary School, MO

Butterflies
I like butterflies.
When they flap their wings they say, "hi."
Flap your wing and you will see it's like you're waving hi to me.
They crawl when they are younger.
When they are big they flitter and flutter.
Butterflies are lots of fun.
Tell me when you see one.
Butterflies have pretty wings.
They can do many things.
I love butterflies and so will you,
I think you already do.

Alyssa Witter, Grade 3
Central Elementary School, WV

A Bouncing Balloon
A balloon is a bird
waiting to be released
bouncing in the air,
a restless balloon.
Let go
so it flies away
flying, flying, flying
and then
it disappears
the balloon is flying...
to the moon!

Meghana Malyala, Grade 3
Hunter GT Magnet Elementary School, NC

Thanksgiving

T oday I feel so grateful,
H oping to share with you;
A lways remembering love
N othing could be so true.
K nowing that God is there,
S preading joy through the air,
G ood things will happen,
I ncredible feelings we'll share.
V isiting our family and friends,
I am sure it will be fun.
N ever our happiness will end,
G iving thanks to everyone!

Lucas Ricardi, Grade 3
Virginia A Boone Highland Oaks Elementary School, FL

Me

Jamesha
Happy, pray, playing
Daughter of Mom and Dad
Who loves Mom, baby, Dad
Who needs water, food, and shelter
Who feels happy, sad, and mad
Who gives friends, mom, and dad
Who fears ghosts, spirits, and Chucky
Who would like to see a movie, Clifford, and my old teacher
Who dreams of Indiana Jones movies, the zoo, and friends
Who lives in a big swing
Springer

Jamesha Springer, Grade 2
Robert E Lee Expressive Arts Elementary School, MO

Hamsters

Hamsters are so fun
They like to eat bun.
I like them because they are funny
But they are such a worry.

They are so quiet and extremely small.
They like to play on the wheel and run with the ball.
They seem like cool pets
One day I will get one yet.

Szymon Taylor, Grade 2
Perrine SDA Elementary School, FL

Fall

In fall
The leaves
Make a breeze.
Red
Makes a bed.
In fall
The trees are tall.
In fall
The squirrels scatter
And chatter.

Gabriella Gray, Grade 2
Eagle's View Academy, FL

The Little Pig

Little pig, little pig
Walked, walked, and walked
Little pig, little pig
Hopped, hopped, and hopped,
Little pig, little pig,
Saw a big wolf.
Little pig, little pig,
Ran, ran, and ran.
Little pig, little pig,
Ran home right then.

Arrington Johnson, Grade 3
Northridge Christian School, OK

My Lion

He didn't roar at anything,
A hyena
A snake
A tall giraffe
A monkey swinging in a tree
A black and white zebra running free
A rhinoceros
A hedgehog
An elephant and an elephant shrew,
He roared at things because he wanted to.

Lexi Welton, Grade 1
Blessed Sacrament School, FL

Addison

I am Addison
Shy, artistic, fun
Child of Anthony and Amy
Who loves snakes
Who needs niceness
Who feels nice
Who gives kindness
Who fears brothers
Who would like to be a scientist
I am Addison

Addison Koch, Grade 3
Lakeland Elementary School, MO

I Want a World Where...

I want a world where...
I am fast as lightning.
My mom is like an angel.
The moon waves at me at night.
The sun dances on my head on a cold day.
The ducks march like a marching band.
I can dive like a dolphin.
My sisters are as sweet as candy.
The weekend is as slow as a turtle.
I want a world where...

Charles Lewis, Grade 3
Rivelon Elementary School, SC

My Bunny

He didn't hop on anything —
A bird
A squirrel
A dish of food
My hairy head
His bumpy bed
A kitchen chair
My sister's lap
My smelly basketball shoe —
He hopped because he wanted to.

Zachariah Steele, Grade 1
Blessed Sacrament School, FL

Imagine a Day…

Imagine a day…
where you were invincible.
You can do anything, go anywhere.
You can't feel anything.

Imagine a day…
where you can do something no one else likes doing.
Something that would hurt them, not you,
like jumping off the Empire State Building
and not feeling anything.

Imagine that.

Jadin Heaston, Grade 3
Robert E Lee Expressive Arts Elementary School, MO

Me

Silvia
Creative, nice, loves animals
Daughter of Mike and Amy Stambaugh
Who loves cats, friends, and art
Who needs warmth, my cat, and family
Who feels happy, sad, excited
Who gives peace, kindness, and hugs
Who fears spiders, snakes, and death
Who would like to see kindness, good friendship, and good teachers
Who dreams of illustrating fun books, friends, and another pet
Who lives in Columbia
Stambaugh

Silvia Stambaugh, Grade 2
Robert E Lee Expressive Arts Elementary School, MO

My Dog Laney's Christmas

My dog likes Christmas
And that's a fact.
She likes to eat a lot
She likes to have a snack!

She plays in the snow.
She chases the cat!
She's glad that I am home,
To scratch her on the back!

Nick Grimm, Grade 1
St Vincent De Paul Elementary School, MO

Butterfly
Very colorful
Flies fast
Looks beautiful
Drinks nectar
Really small
Butterfly

Diana Feier, Grade 2
Ponte Vedra Palm Valley Elementary School, FL

Recess
It looks like freedom,
It sounds like wind,
It feels like home,
It tastes like nature,
It smells breezy,
And everything is fun.

Phineas Lehan, Grade 2
Ponte Vedra Palm Valley Elementary School, FL

Cake
I like how it tastes.
I like the batter before it bakes.
I always get it all over my face.
My favorite flavor is chocolate but I like others too.
The icing on top is delicious as well.
I like all kinds of colors from brown to dark blue.

Kelsey Goss, Grade 2
Bramlett Elementary School, GA

Singing
I have a beautiful voice.
I can sing for the Lord.
I hope to sing from the stage.
So I can bring joy and peace.

Cameron Strachan, Grade 2
James E Sampson Memorial Adventist School, FL

Ants
Ants are cool like food.
Ants are as tiny as dust.
Ants are cute like leaves.

Annette Ng, Grade 2
Virginia A Boone Highland Oaks Elementary School, FL

The Zoo

The zoo is full of monkeys.
The zoo is full of donkeys.

The giraffe has a long neck.
Watch out the birds will give you a peck.

The rhinoceros is big and black.
And the lions will attack.

I can spend all day at the zoo
as long as I have food to chew.

Beres Strachan, Grade 2
James E Sampson Memorial Adventist School, FL

Picnics

Picnics are a lot of fun,
that's why I invited everyone.

Mom packed a lot of lunch
that's good because we need a bunch.

Dad is starting up the car
we are going very far.

Everyone had lots of fun.
We played until the day was done.

Ananda Glover, Grade 3
James E Sampson Memorial Adventist School, FL

Grandpa Ross

Sweet and nice Grandpa
I watch him get older by the day
He always lets me sit on his lap
His warm arms wrap around me
His smile so BIG and WIDE

One year later he let Alzheimer's get the best of him
He will always be in my heart

Grandpa, you are the best to me!

Emma Steedly, Grade 3
Buckner Elementary School, KY

Lindsey Is My Best Friend for Life
Lindsey
beautiful, sweet
dances, runs, flips
you can do it!
Linzy bug
Riley Pirkle, Grade 3
Briarwood Christian School, AL

Emily Lane
Emily Lane
flexible, funky
runs, kicks, scores
she is super fast!
soccer girl
Emily Lane Ray, Grade 3
Briarwood Christian School, AL

Noah
Noah
fun, sweet
runs, plays, prays
wow! that is cool
Tiger
Noah Whatley, Grade 3
Briarwood Christian School, AL

Baseball Star
Shane Victorino
tough, talented
plays outfield, hits, runs
he is really good!
#9
Ben Splawn, Grade 3
Briarwood Christian School, AL

Sarah S.
Sarah
beautiful, kind
cheers, runs, sings
that is so cool!
Shae-shae
Brooke McGehee, Grade 3
Briarwood Christian School, AL

Gregory
Gregory
creative, clever
plays, dashes, constructs
I am so happy!
child
Gregory Giles, Grade 3
Briarwood Christian School, AL

Basketball Hero
Michael Jordan
amazing, strong
dunks, shoots, leaps
fast, tough, moves, famous
Air Jordan
Mason Byrd, Grade 3
Briarwood Christian School, AL

Kai
Kai
cool, humble
happy, runs, football
be very Godly
Ki, Ky, Tie
Kai Frederick, Grade 3
Briarwood Christian School, AL

Justin
Justin
kind, caring
soccer, scouts, reading
I'm friends with everyone
J.J.
Justin Jett, Grade 3
Briarwood Christian School, AL

Beautiful Ballet
Beautiful
graceful, leaps
skips, points, smiles
fun, athletic, gracefully, pretty
Ballerina
Chandler Coshatt, Grade 3
Briarwood Christian School, AL

Animals Off Vacation

Moving black ball, as you touch it water
Dripping down on your hands, rolling on your hand
Beaming down on your forehead like hot water on a hot day
Smelled like poo, soggy, wet, stinky.
Touching the rail, sweat in between our own hands
Walk turning into a run, running on a down hill
Sweat dripping down your face, d r i p d r o p on the floor
You're walking down your sister spots a gecko, running after the gecko
Your sister is going running faster and faster than you
Stopping her, your cousin's mom yelling, "COME BACK NOW!"
Your sister running slowly turning into a walk
Now going into the reptile section.
Look at the snake looking back at your cousin's brother
He's crying because the snakes are licking their lips
You're saying "Charlie it's OK"
Him going under into a deep sleep
We are begging to eat, we find a picnic table with a pond
"Ducks" we all say. You say…"Oh no."
Eating sandwiches and some Pringles. "Yummy," you say.
After 4 to 5 hours you take a bite. "Mmmmmm."
Moving on to a different section. Fish.

Madison Williams, Grade 3
Camden Station Elementary School, KY

The Rules of Baseball

This little story needs telling to all,
Since it's about me, a bat, and a ball.
It's a game that can be played under the stars,
Everywhere you can play it, even on Mars.

Yes, you got it right — baseball's the sport,
And all can play, whether you are tall or short.
Hitting, running, and fielding are important skills,
And hearing the crowd cheer can give you the chills.

Everyone tries their very best to score,
But there's one rule of the game that can't be ignored.
Winning isn't everything, although it may seem,
The most important thing is to act as a team.

Cameron Feldman, Grade 3
Virginia A Boone Highland Oaks Elementary School, FL

Thanksgiving

Oh, how we give thanks on Thanksgiving!
We thank all the people who served our
    Country,
And thought of us.

Oh, how we give thanks on Thanksgiving!
It is such a special holiday.
You should give thanks every day as on
    Thanksgiving.

Oh, how we give thanks on Thanksgiving!
We celebrate with the family on
    Thanksgiving.
So, give thanks on Thanksgiving!
    Raychel Harves, Grade 3
    St Paul's Lutheran School, OK

Kaitlyn

I have a little beige dog.
He's cute from head to toe.
His name is King
But he can't sing.

He likes to play around the house.
And jumps up on the bed.
He catches the mouse.
Then lays it on the floor.

I love him dearly.
He's good to me.
King is a true friend.
The best dog ever.
    Kaitlyn Taylor, Grade 2
    Perrine SDA Elementary School, FL

I Love Pizza

My name is Emma.
I love to eat pizza.
I only like cheese on it.
I would eat it every day.
I love pizza.
    Emma Snipes, Grade 1
    Oakland Primary School, SC

Yummy Fall

Fall is yummy!
Yes, it is!
When I come in the kitchen
I smell pumpkin pie.
Pulping the pumpkin
Is so much fun!
I can have fun with you.
Apple cider
What a great drink
To gulp down in fall.
In the fall
Leaves tumble down the trees.
You can feel the breeze.
The wind picks them up
Like an airplane.
    Whitney Ward, Grade 3
    Eagle's View Academy, FL

Birthday

Paper planes gliding in the air.
Running, jumping, yelling
Cake, pizza, soda
Presents!
Rip, tear, throwing
Paper
Reading letters
Jumping all around.
Cake on the floor
Slipping, falling
Everybody out
The door
Stomp,
Stomp,
Stomp.
    Jake Dziedzic, Grade 3
    Camden Station Elementary School, KY

Mary Morgan

Sing, likes to play
dance, watch TV, laugh at brother
because I am nice to them
    Guin Renfroe, Grade 3
    Briarwood Christian School, AL

Butterfly

Butterfly flying as fast as the ocean.
Waves rushing close by.
Running after you.
Butterfly twirling like a ballerina.
Swaying like a flower in the crystal wind.
Rushing through the crystal wind.
RUNNING
Wind shining like a diamond

S

  h

    i

      n

        i

          n

            g

Shining like the daisy sun.
Cassidy Weidekamp, Grade 3
Buckner Elementary School, KY

Jingle Bells

Jingle bells are yellow,
They might sound quite mellow.
Here the cling, cling, cling,
from that thing, thing, thing.
The bells are made of gold.
They are priceless I am told.
Chad Moody, Grade 2
Macon-East Montgomery Academy, AL

Florida

Water the water glares at me with a smile.
Sandy beaches.
Enjoyable.
Peninsula.
South and far from Kentucky.

The waves pummel up to
Shore.
Florida is great

Florida is remarkable.
Cody Grasch, Grade 3
Camden Station Elementary School, KY

The Scare of the Bear

You must be aware of the bear
Eating your hair.
He is such a little bear
To be eating your hair.

I would not dare to get a bear,
Because he will eat your hair
Because he's a bear.
So you must be aware of the bears.

They made a care for bears to learn
Not to eat peoples' hair,
But you still have to be aware of the bears,
Because they might still eat your hair.

Some of the bears have escaped.

The bears care
But the bears aren't eating peoples' hair,
So bears' care helps bears learn,
To not eat people's hair.

People now have bears for pets
To eat the hair
That falls off onto the floor.
Haley Jameson, Grade 3
Charles Towne Montessori School, SC

Grandparents

G ood fisherman
R eally good cook
A lways watching fishing on TV
N ice to take walks with
D rinks ice tea
P lays board games with me
A merica lover
R etired from the airport
E ating her fried potatoes
N ever inactive
T akes me hunting
S ometimes we go camping
Kirby Williams, Grade 3
Clinton Christian Academy, MO

Bear
Big, ferocious
Wild, crazy
Eats meat
Is scary
Sharp teeth
Run for
Your life!

Skylie Shields, Grade 2
Ponte Vedra Palm Valley Elementary School, FL

Emily
Emily is like a sister to me, she has a warm heart and smile, her smiles sparkles
like a star,
Emily has twinkling blue eyes, she has sparkling blond hair that twinkles in the sun,
Emily makes my heart warm up when she hugs me even if I'm down,
she makes my heart and smile warm up when I see her,
EMILY!

Molly Dean, Grade 3
Camden Station Elementary School, KY

Butterflies
I wish that I was a colorful butterfly.
The ones that are the same colors as the beautiful rainbows in the sky.
I see them flying up and down and left and right.
Excitement and joy is what I see in my sight.
The butterflies are flying all day.
It makes me ask, "Can I go your way?"

Crystal Cooper, Grade 1
Oakland Primary School, SC

My Dog
It looks furry.
It sounds barky.
It feels soft like a cover.
It tastes like wet soil.
It smells like soil.
I love dogs!

Vera Robinson, Grade 2
Ponte Vedra Palm Valley Elementary School, FL

Leaping Frog
Diving in the water
As the rushing creak rumbles
The leaping frogs leap to a rock

Jump and jump
Hopping down
In the pond

Hopping around like a frog
On a lily pad
And on the rock

He goes on a lily pad
Jumping around in the grass.
Abigail Stucker, Grade 2
Buckner Elementary School, KY

Family
My father is my heart.
I love him; he's the best.
He works.
He protects me
He loves me, too.

My mom is my soul.
She cooks, cleans, and teaches.
She's the best mom ever.

My sister and brothers
Help me; teach me.
I love them.
They love me, too.
Hannah Poirier, Grade 3
Caneview Elementary School, LA

I Like Cars
Cars are fun
Cars are fast
I have lots of cars
They are big and small
I like cars.
Landon Nicholson, Grade 1
Oakland Primary School, SC

Sports
I like sports.
Any kind of sports.
Throwing sports, hitting sports,
Running sports, kicking sports.
Sports on courts.
Sports on fields.
Sports with balls.
Any kind of sports.
I like sports.
Preston Thrasher, Grade 3
Landmark Christian School, GA

I Like...
I like movies.
Any kind of movies.
Slow movies, fast movies,
Loud movies, silent movies.
Movies in a house.
Movies on a TV.
Movies with Scooby Doo.
Any kind of movies.
I like movies.
Jada Anderson, Grade 3
Landmark Christian School, GA

Football
Tyrone Prothro
plays for Alabama, wide receiver
catches, runs, scores
my time is here
wide catcher
Walter Vetrano, Grade 3
Briarwood Christian School, AL

JoJo
I know a bird named JoJo.
He is very cute.
He sings very pretty.
We could do a melody.
When I look at him I think of the sky.
I love JoJo!
Addison Toy, Grade 2
Evangelical Christian School, TN

Cats
Cats cats cats
I love cats
Some cats are fluffy some cats are funny
Some cats love play
Some cats love to sleep almost all day
Brown cats orange cats
and all the other colored cats

Cats such independent creatures
Their meow so gentle and mellow
It sounds like music in my ear
Their rich coats like precious art work
with designs so beautiful
Their stripes going left to right
Oh cats I LOVE you

When they're not in the mood
scratch scratch
They'll give you a boo-boo
Cats cats cats
I LOVE cats!

Alexis Taylor, Grade 3
Virginia A Boone Highland Oaks Elementary School, FL

My Rats
Winter white
Midnight black.
Going right to left,
Down   up.
Down   up
Down next up
Tiny feet as cold, as the north pole on my palm.

Quiet when asleep.
Crunch,   crunch,   crunch,
On delicious food.

Ch'ing, ch'ing, ch'ing, in the cage,
At night.
My eyes pop open again!

Carson Strunk, Grade 2
Buckner Elementary School, KY

My Special Bunny Blanket

It's special as can be,
the cute bunnies playing with toys.
Blue and pink pajamas on their sweet brown fur,

Bunnies are ready for bed,
you give a good night kiss and tuck them in.
They close their eyes and fall asleep,
faster than you can think.

The soft fuzzy blanket fabric on my face.
Fuzzy like stuffing in fake animals,
the sweet smell in my nose.

When I'm gone I wonder what it does?

When I'm gone I think it is asleep
or listens to my radio.
It might play my DS
but I think it thinks of me.
I love my bunny blanket.
It is special as can be!

Dani Jerome, Grade 3
Camden Station Elementary School, KY

Holidays

Autumn is the time of year, when you start to feel a chill.
The leaves are turning orange and gold, pretty soon it will be cold.
Outside I hear the sound of rain,
Trickling down the window pane.
Inside the house it's warm and nice.
I can smell the scent of pine and the fireplace is bright.
Candles glowing all around,
I love this season's sights and sounds.

On Thanksgiving, the scent of cinnamon apples fills the air,
The dressing is a little dry, but I don't care.
The turkey is ready, it's juicy and plump
And there will be plenty to fill me up.
There is cranberry sauce to my dismay,
but I love pumpkin pie, I can eat it every day!

Sheadon Moncree, Grade 3
S Ray Lowder Elementary School, NC

Just Like Me
There is pie
There are pumpkins
There is pumpkin pie.
It is sweet.
It is orange.
It is good...
Just like me
And just like you.
There are flowers
There are people
There is the sun
There are clouds
There is me.
Sarah Caudle, Grade 2
Richmond Elementary School, OK

I Am Thankful
I am thankful for me
and I am thankful for my mom
because she likes to cook.
I am thankful for my body.
It moves like an angel,
fast and slow.
I like to run and feel the hard floor
or sit on the soft couch.
I love the seasons,
the trees that give us oxygen
and help us to breathe.
I am thankful for love.
It is the best thing to give.
Cierre Wesley, Grade 2
Lee A Tolbert Community Academy, MO

The Holy Angel
The holy angel is bright and holy

And a guardian of God.
Gloriful
And truthful
And sounds beautiful

Strong in the Lord,
Wonderful
A messenger
Glorious and generous

The holy angel is good hearted
Andy Cruver, Grade 3
Landmark Christian School, GA

My Hard Life
Oh, my hard life.
How I bring in the wood.
Oh, my hard life.
And I vacuum the floor.
Oh, my hard life.
Can I do any more?
Oh, my hard life.
As I find my own clothes.
Oh, my hard life.
When I fold my clothes.
I wonder how I do my hard life
But I'm still surprised that I can
Do all that I do.
Robert Gregory III, Grade 3
Carver Elementary School, NC

My Pets
I had three dogs,
Two died,
I miss them.
One ran away.
I had two cats,
One died,
The other ran away.
Niehaimah K. Gibbs, Grade 1
Cool Spring Elementary School, NC

The Snow Is Falling
The snow is falling the snow is falling
the snow is falling today.
I got to ride on my sleigh!
The snow is falling today
and I always build snowmen.
and winter will be gone
I will be so sad.
Ruby Cunningham, Grade 1
Riverhill School, AL

Rip in My Pants
I go to the store with my mom and I hear a rip and a zip.
And the people at the store said ha-ha-ha
and I run home and get a new pair of pants.
Then my mom said I didn't get all my groceries
so we go back to the store to get the groceries
and rip zip we go back home and I get a new pair of pants so I get a belt
and go to the store and this time no rip or zip.

Bradon Long, Grade 3
Columbia Catholic School, MO

Life
The summer is gone.
Arid winds are rising.
I see an image of an artistic picture in my mind.
It has mountains and elks that are leaving on the horizon.
Is there any skyscraper that the heavens can't meet?
Can my stone cold heart skip a beat?
I will live my life as a mystery.

Savannah Gillelan, Grade 3
Love Memorial Elementary School, NC

Army
Jeep
green, rugged
driving, fighting, carrying supplies
army, four wheels, people on top, eleven wheels
driving, fighting, shooting
camouflage, big
Tank

Tyler Keim, Grade 3
St Joseph Institute for the Deaf, MO

Halloween
Kids running with tons of candy in their bags.
Scaring and scaring
Zombies, ghosts, and monsters and all kinds of costumes
Eating your candy
Your mom said let's go and you say come on
Just a couple more minutes please OK
And you go get more candy

Cole Mesker, Grade 3
Buckner Elementary School, KY

Bananas

Bananas, bananas
We love bananas
Banana pudding
Banana bread
Banana muffins
Banana ice cream
Bananas, bananas
We love bananas
So good and healthy.

Haley Maine, Grade 1
Cool Spring Elementary School, NC

I'm Me

I am a fine blue.
You don't see me every day.
I'm the ocean,
very strong and active.
I have lots of friends.
I never give up.
My mind is stronger than me.
My mind makes the coral in the sea,
But I'm just me.

Maddie Solodky, Grade 3
Sabal Point Elementary School, FL

We Give Thanks on Christmas

On Christmas morning we wake up,
We wake our mom and dad.
We open up our presents,
We are very glad.
We give thanks on Christmas,
We go to church and pray.
We give thanks to God,
It is an awesome day!

Cooper Nelson, Grade 1
Westlake Christian School, FL

Flight Night

A bat
Will ever try to fly
As the moon shines.

J'Vion Boutte, Grade 3
Caneview Elementary School, LA

Decorating for Christmas

We can decorate Christmas trees,
We get them from outside.
We put a star on the top,
Under the tree, the presents hide.
We put up Christmas lights,
Our train lights up, too.
The lights are pretty,
My favorites are blue.

Michael Wakefield, Grade 1
Westlake Christian School, FL

Snowmen Are Cool

You can make a snowman,
You can make it with snow.
You add branches and a carrot,
That's what I know.
Christmas trees are green,
They have a star on top.
You put ornaments on them,
You find them at the Santa Shop.

Jackson Imlah, Grade 1
Westlake Christian School, FL

About Me

My name is Price and I am tall.
I like all kinds of balls.
I like to play Wii.
Would you play with me?
I have a friend, Ethan.
He is my best friend.
He likes me, I like him too.

Price Turner, Grade 1
Evangelical Christian School, TN

Day and Night

I like day, you like night.
You want to know why?
I like day because you can play.
I really wonder why you don't like day.
I still like you even if you don't like day.
I will always like you.

Anniston Napier, Grade 3
Alpena Elementary School, AR

Super Pumpkin
I have a little pumpkin,
His name is Superboy!
When I say, "Let's go!"
He'll start to fly!
He then tells me what to buy!
"Toys for me," he will say,
Or he'll fly away!
Super pumpkin, why won't you come back?
You have a good personality. And super hearing too!
And everyone would really like to see just you!
Come back please!

Austin Doolittle, Grade 3
Coral Springs Elementary School, FL

Night Flight
Gray foxes run wildly across the street.
Orange kittens are afraid they'll be dead meat.

Blue fish swim away.
Brown sharks want to play.

Black bears dance all night.
White striped skunks cause a fright.

Silver moonlight brings trouble near.
Golden rays make it all disappear.

Ethan Britt, Grade 3
Evangel Christian Academy, AL

Predictions for the Future
In the future I predict
new foods will be grown and picked.

Robots will play jacks
and kids will fly jet packs.

Rainbows will have more coloration
and we'll go to space for vacation.

All these things are in my sight.
Wait and see if I am right.

Olivia Gottlieb, Grade 3
Virginia A Boone Highland Oaks Elementary School, FL

Pumpkin Munchkin

Pumpkin Munchkin as cute as can be.
I treat him like a baby!
He's very shy,
I'm not going to lie.
He really likes apple pie!
He loves to look at the blue, blue sky.
He loves the feeling when you tickle his feet.
Isn't this a pumpkin, you'd like to meet?

Kayla Butler, Grade 3
Coral Springs Elementary School, FL

The Secret

This Christmas I will whisper
In Santa's ear.
I will tell him something
I want him to hear!
I would like a puppy.
He should be all black.
Please Santa bring him!!!
Put him in your pack!

Tommy Taylor, Grade 1
St Vincent De Paul Elementary School, MO

Rain Falls

Click clack it hits the roofs of people's houses
Sometimes rain sounds like a knock on the door
you come, you open the door
no one's there just dripping rain. Drip drop
Little water droplets
dropping from the puffy cotton ball clouds
puddles filled with clear water
RAIN!!!!

Tom Brown, Grade 3
Camden Station Elementary School, KY

SpongeBob

SpongeBob is a square.
SpongeBob is yellow.
SpongeBob has a lot of wholes in his yellow belly.
SpongeBob is friendly.
And SpongeBob likes to wear white underwear.

Eric Singleton II, Grade 1
Oakland Primary School, SC

Radiant Flowers
Yellow flowers
Shine like the bright blazing hot sun.
Cold light autumn air
Rustles
Leaves.
Delicate smooth petals
Float off
The dark green stems.

Flowers
Glitter and sparkle
While swaying side to side.
Pink, purple, and red flowers
Bump into each other.

As wind whirls around and around
Like a tornado.
Flowers dance

To the ZOOMING wind.

Anna Wells, Grade 3
Buckner Elementary School, KY

Football
I love to play football all the time.
It is worth more than a dime.

When I get tackled I'll get back up
The next time I hope I don't fall on a cup.

When I run I run fast
Then I get to the goal last.

I feel bad when I'm not in the game.
When I get in other might feel the same.

When the quarterback hands off the ball.
The halfback tries to score and not fall.

Finally the game is over
Now I can play with my dog Rover.

Travon Ross, Grade 3
James E Sampson Memorial Adventist School, FL

Thanksgiving Day

I taste
The turkey still sizzling from the oven
The warm cookies melting in my mouth
The chicken stew burning my tongue

I see
The nice turkey, family, and friends at the dinner table

I smell
My mom's macaroni and cheese coming out of the oven
My aunt making cookies
My grandmother getting out the cranberry sauce

I hear
My cousin making asparagus casserole
My dad and grandfather smoking the turkey
All my friends and family talking loudly

I feel
Delightfully happy and glad that all my friends and family
Are sitting at the dinner table together

I know
Thanksgiving is great in all different ways

Charlotte Koonce, Grade 3
Riverhill School, AL

Wondering

Walking in a big spacy room
With a burst of sun shining in the glass door.
Air, dust and crumbs,
Are the only things there.
So soft carpets,
Short and long strips of wood
Stretch across.
Weeds spring from the ground
A perfect view
Standing like a statue on the deck,
Staring and...
Wondering
If this is our house.

Michael Aubrey, Grade 3
Camden Station Elementary School, KY

Candy
pop rocks jumping in my mouth
sugary, sweet lollipops and suckers
can't wait to open the wrapper.
sticky lollipops and suckers
chocolate water fall flowing through my mouth
chocolate melting in my mouth.
candy rocks!

Jacob Justice, Grade 2
Buckner Elementary School, KY

Butterflies
I love butterflies big ones and small ones too.
Many butterflies' wings are white and black, yellow and black
or orange, white and black.
Butterflies laid their eggs on leaves
and a caterpillar comes out of the eggs
and turns into a butterfly that comes out of a chrysalis.
What is your favorite butterfly?

Sheldine Bonne-Annee, Grade 3
Virginia A Boone Highland Oaks Elementary School, FL

My Favorite Season
Spring is great.
You see pretty flowers.
Picking them will help you pass the hours.
Friends come when you want to play.
I wish spring was every day.
Summer, fall and winter are all ok,
Because I know spring is on the way.

Tori Derise, Grade 3
Caneview Elementary School, LA

Basketball
I love basketball.
I love how the backboard makes a "BAM!" sound when the ball hits it.
I love when the crowd goes wild when someone makes a slam dunk.
I love the sound of the buzzer when it goes off.
I love it when the orange as a tiger ball goes flying through the air to celebrate
winning the game.
I love when my team high fives me when I make the winning shot.

Aidan Sullivan, Grade 3
Hunter GT Magnet Elementary School, NC

Writer's Block
Eyes focused
Frustrated
Confused
Mind lost
Pencil ready
Fingers tapping
Staring
No idea
Talk to teacher
Idea struck brain
Writing
Full paper
MORE paper
DONE!

Joshua Hicks, Grade 3
Hunter GT Magnet Elementary School, NC

Snowflakes
Snowflakes falling from the sky
creating a frosty white desert below
covering the gentle green
spreading colds far and near

Sitting inside
waiting
for the treacherous white
to ride away

But then
there are hills to sled down
and games to be won
in the snow.

Ben Goldman, Grade 3
Hunter GT Magnet Elementary School, NC

Spring Time
It looks like the wind going through my hair.
It sounds like birds chirping.
It feels like a soft bird landing on me.
It smells like a blooming flower.
I think spring is perfect!

Anna Lube, Grade 2
Ponte Vedra Palm Valley Elementary School, FL

Autumn

A ll the leaves are falling
U nexpected wind
T he leaves are crackling under my boots
U nbeatable cherry pie
M any good aromas
N asty ham makes my tummy feel disgusting

Tristan Taveras, Grade 3
Central Park Elementary School, FL

Water

Trickling over the edge.
Transparent droplets splashing out at me.
Moving along quickly, quietly and softly
Leaves dropping in and fluttering past.
Quiet gurgles of water as I pass a tiny trickling waterfall
Running along a soft but soothing melody of peace.

Brendan Conroy, Grade 3
Camden Station Elementary School, KY

Raining Leaves

It's raining leaves.
It's raining leaves.
It's pulling me away.
It feels like I'm floating on a cloud way above you.
It feels like I'm on a soft bed in the clouds.
It feels like my head is melting into the cloud.

Madison Montross, Grade 3
Camden Station Elementary School, KY

Don't Do Drugs

Don't do drugs because your eyes will get red.
You don't need to smoke at all so don't do drugs.
If you do drugs your life won't be the same as it was.
Always say "no" to drugs.

Alonna McCollum, Grade 2
Mount Olive Elementary School, MS

Iguanas

Iguanas are cool.
They jump off rocks like a frog.
I love iguanas.

Ali Levy, Grade 2
Virginia A Boone Highland Oaks Elementary School, FL

A Day at the Field
"Get ready,
For the coin toss,"
The white cap bellows.
"TAILS!" the other team says.

"You're Heads you're Tails"
Squirming, like worms
"Heads" "KICK."

The ball blasting
Through the air and
"Go,"
Shouts, the carrier blasting
Through the wall,
"Hit Hard FUMBLE"
The commentator says
In a bellowing voice
Gripping the scaly skin the Chargers have it.
Breaks 1, 2 and 3 tackles with a touchdown
Chargers feeling like a savior
Way to put some pig in the house.

Noah McKinley, Grade 3
Buckner Elementary School, KY

The Night When Santa Came
The night that Santa came
The snow was very deep.
I didn't even hear him
He didn't make a peep.

While we were sleeping
He came to our tree
He came a creeping
He left presents for me!

He ate all the cookies.
He drank all the milk.
He left our house night
And continued his flight!

Victor Thomas, Grade 1
St Vincent De Paul Elementary School, MO

Where I'm From

I am from berries from bushes,
nuggets, apples, pies, pudding,
mashed potatoes, chicken rings, cheese pizza,
grilled steaks, fried apple pies.

I am from hide-and-go-seek, Monopoly,
Wii Fit, Nintendo D.S., Game Boy, tag, house,
Mouse Trap, computer games, Pokémon,
cards, pillow fighting, hop scotch.
I am from soccer balls, cooking, writing, reading,
shopping, baseball, kickball, volleyball

I am from Mom, Dad, JoJo,
Serenty, Nicole, Corey, Jillan, Cruz,
Megan, Sophie, The Emily's, Leigh Ann,
Ronnye Jo, Morgan, Trinity

I am from Wendy's McDonald's,
Calvary Church, Alvaton School, ball games
Pensacola Beach

I am from riding bikes, stuffed animals,
roller blades, costumes, hats, *Race to Witch Mountain*, Junie B. Jones' books.

Maddy McCorkle, Grade 3
Alvaton Elementary School, KY

Autumn Sounds

When I go outside in the autumn I hear
Lots of different sounds all around in the air.
When the wind blows, leaves on trees rustle.
They fall to the ground and hardly
Make a sound.
Sometimes I hear
The rain pitter patter.
Puddles grow
As rain drops fall.
I hear acorns falling,
As they plop to the ground.
When night comes hundreds of very loud
Crickets chirp to one another.

Emma Rasmussen, Grade 3
Westminster Christian Academy, GA

The Lost Dog
There was a little dog
He was lost
He walked along the street
And he was scared
It was dark and he heard scary noises
He looked around as his body shook in fear
And standing there
To save his life
Was the only person he wanted to be near
His best friend, his owner
Was there to take him home.

Adrian Ureno, Grade 2
Kerr Elementary School, OK

Christmas
While kids are fast asleep
Dreaming of huge presents
Santa flies through the towns
Carrying an enormous bag of presents.

His reindeer clop on the roof.
Santa slides down the chimney with his bag.
He spreads the presents around the trees,
he eats cookies and drinks milk.
When he gets back up he feeds the reindeer carrots
Elves are out looking for good children.

Andrew Campbell, Grade 3
Camden Station Elementary School, KY

Flowers
Pretty colors
Swaying beautifully
Back, forth
Up, down
Green stem
Growing stronger
Every day
Freshening air
Cleaning soil
Helping animals
Spreading seeds.

Sarah Fraga, Grade 2
Ponte Vedra Palm Valley Elementary School, FL

A Wild Ride!
Waiting in a *huge* line
you say
"hurry up" but nobody does

You're looking happy to be going on the outside
But
on the inside
you're a little afraid

People screaming
louder than dynamite
exploding
close by

Going faster and faster
screaming as loud as you can

And just as you conquer
the petrifying hills
and the huge thrills
and of course the devilish loops
it screeches to a halt
and you wonder why you were so afraid
Lindsay Harris, Grade 3
Camden Station Elementary School, KY

I Am a Dragon
I am a dragon and I mean no harm
I will not bite off your arm.
I shoot fire, but I don't suck on a pacifier
I'm saying again I mean no harm!
I live on a dragon farm.
I have spikes, I love kites.
I chew on toys, so boys pick up your toys!
I spit and slobber, but I don't mean to bother.
I want a balloon
I like to look at the moon
I burned a castle, and I like to wrestle.
I'm purple and black, so stay back!
I mean no harm,
And I promise I will not bite off your arm!
Jeremee Buller, Grade 3
Hillsdale Christian School, OK

The Wolf in My Backyard

There's a wolf in my backyard,
Maybe it's standing guard,
I'll go look in my neighbor's backyard.
Look! Another gray wolf!
And now it's standing guard.

The wolf-pups are not too far,
They're in the trunk of mom's car,
Now they're coming to meet together.
They're eating berries in fall weather.

Julia Boeyink, Grade 2
Spoede Elementary School, MO

Memories

Memories are something that was old
and you still love it.
Memories are kept in your mind
because nobody can take them.
Memories are funny
because they make you laugh.
Memories make me thankful
because I can remember
that I appreciate my family,
my school, and a teacher.

Anthony Yancy, Grade 2
Lee A Tolbert Community Academy, MO

The Curtain

The curtain flows
way down low.
To my feet
oh that lovely sheet.
The satin lines that I designed.
Oh that is clearly mine.
I love my curtain for that is certain
that my curtain can fly.
But I think it is time to say
good-bye.

Nova Cunningham, Grade 3
Norris Childers Elementary School, NC

The Halloween Day

It's Halloween!
Let's all celebrate.
We all get ready to go outside
and see the leaves.
We take some pictures,
Then head out trick or treating.
We get so much candy
We can't even eat it.
Let's go home now,
We have to get ready for next Halloween.

Keri Montagnino, Grade 3
Cool Spring Elementary School, NC

Scooby Doo

S haggy's friend
C onstantly hungry
O pen mouth
O nion rings
B urgers with cheese
Y ikes ghost

D og who's funny
O lives that are green
O ther foods

Gracie Bolton, Grade 3
Landmark Christian School, GA

Halloween

I like Halloween
Because it's scary.
It is not hairy.
Or is it?
No, it's not.
Sometimes when we knock on the door
They lock the door.
But when they don't,
They open the door.
We go, "BOO!"

Jordan Bailie, Grade 3
Eagle's View Academy, FL

I Like…

I like games,
Any kind of games,
Long games, advanced games,
Video games, board games,
Games in a box,
Games on a shelf,
Games with action,
Any kinds of games
I like games.

Bryce Williamson, Grade 3
Landmark Christian School, GA

Toys

I like toys.
Any kind of toys.
Big toys, small toys,
Cool toys, lame toys.
Toys in a box
Toys on a dresser
Toys with accessories
Any kind of toys.
I like toys.

Gator Wallace, Grade 3
Landmark Christian School, GA

Best Friends Forever

Chandler
sweet, fun
ballet, run, cartwheels
"wear pigtails this week"
Cece

Sarah Stephenson, Grade 3
Briarwood Christian School, AL

Vacation

I am going on a vacation destination.
Waves hit the beach
With a splash.
Later, silent and quiet;
I lay down
And watch the sunset.

Makenna Landry, Grade 3
Caneview Elementary School, LA

Christmas

Christmas, Christmas is coming soon!
Watch out for Santa.
Leave him lots of cookies
And milk by the chimney.

Go, Go, Go to sleep
And don't make a peep.
Ho! Ho! Merry Christmas!
Santa has come.

Shaniya Pernell, Grade 3
Carver Elementary School, NC

Christmas

C hrist
H appy
R eindeer
I ncredible
S o good
T reats
M any presents
A wesome
S anta

Ethan Humphrey, Grade 3
Landmark Christian School, GA

Splish, Splash

swimming
exercise, splash
diving, cannonball, freestyle
towels, sun, scuba, goggles
breaststroke

Brady Lehane, Grade 3
Briarwood Christian School, AL

A Summer Day

The sky is blue.
Clouds are white.
The sun is bright.
I like to ride my bike.
Give me a kite
and I will take it for a flight.

Cody Jones, Grade 1
Oakland Primary School, SC

Star

Star sparkles in the night,
Shiny, lovely, goldish yellow,
Nice
A little whisper
Barely heard
Tastes like a cookie,
Smells like a star,
Appears tiny, but not really tiny
Stays close to a planet
Beautiful
Jacob Just-Buddy, Grade 3
Landmark Christian School, GA

My Mom

You are very smart
You have a big heart

You fill me with love
I know you are from up above

No matter where you are
You will always shine
Like a shining star
Payton Buchanan, Grade 3
A H Watwood Elementary School, AL

Butterflies

Butterflies in the air
They fly every day
They get pollen every day
Always get it, they never stop
They fly every day in a pretty way
Abigail Player, Grade 1
Oakland Primary School, SC

My Puppy

My puppy wears a dress.
My puppy eats food that's red.
My puppy is black and brown.
My puppy never ever frowns.
My puppy goes to bed.
Shimarya Martin, Grade 1
Oakland Primary School, SC

I See

I see a bird.
I see a tree.
I see a fly.
I see a bee.
What do you see?
Julia Brody, Grade 1
Oakland Primary School, SC

The Race

A boy wants to race.
He ran too fast.
I couldn't catch up.
He won the race.
I won second place.
Tony Raymond, Grade 1
Oakland Primary School, SC

The Cat

The cat
Smelled a rat
The rat ran
Back to its house sick
So he made some soup in a pan
Emma Siratt, Kindergarten
Northeast Baptist School, LA

Snowman

I sit in my window watching the snow.
Snow falls and falls.
I can't wait to play in the snow.
Snow falls and falls.
I can make a snowman.
DeMonte Tevis, Grade 1
Oakland Primary School, SC

My Sister

I have a new sister.
Her name is Danielle.
I help Mommy with her.
She is tiny.
I love her.
Layla Kelly, Grade 1
Oakland Primary School, SC

Beauty Is

Beauty is…

a sunrise and a sunset,
kittens and babies,
my Mommy, my sister, and my Mimi,
flowers,
my house when it's Christmastime
new clothes just for me,
my toothless grin,
new friends,
snow and mountains,
and the turtle in the lake behind my house.
That's what beauty is to me.

Skylar Blinn, Grade 1
Altermese S Bentley Elementary School, FL

Me

Charlie
Fun, cool, funny
Daughter of Jennifer and Chris
Who loves Mom, Dad, and art
Who needs love, friends, and pets
Who feels sad, happy, and mad
Who gives presents, hugs, and high fives
Who fears ghosts, sharks, and vampires
Who would like to see the oceans, happy people, and good friends
Who dreams of a shark eating me, pigs, and choking
Who lives in Columbia
Perlow-Stevens

Charlie Perlow-Stevens, Grade 2
Robert E Lee Expressive Arts Elementary School, MO

Lunch

Picking
Eating
Munching
Chomping
Destroying
Leaving

Lunch

Jaden Reitzer, Grade 2
Ponte Vedra Palm Valley Elementary School, FL

Going Fishing
Black and gray fish
Jumping out of the water
Throwing our line

Out like a baseball
Pulling it in like
A fish
Swimming in the water

On the bank
No fish on the line
Throwing it out
Like a jet flying in the air
I got a big one Dad

It was a big wet flapping bass
I felt good
Because I haven't caught a big fish
In my whole life.
Brandon Colyer, Grade 3
Buckner Elementary School, KY

Papa
I can still feel his
Cold hands
Touching my now cozy body.

As sunshine gets
To my heart

he says I love you
in his deep voice.

I love standing there
Having my
Hands wrapped around
Him as he asks,
"Where's my sugar?"

Every time I see him
He is my treasure
I love seeing his handsome smile.
Zoë Sanford, Grade 3
Buckner Elementary School, KY

Dogs Like Love Birds
Dogs so happy
Dogs so sad
Dogs bark when danger or robber is here
Cheer you up
When you're
D
O
W
N
Bring love to your heart
Dogs like love birds
Dogs so cute
Dogs so cuddly
Dogs like love birds
Dogs make you happy
Dogs make you sad
Dogs play with you when you're lonely
Dogs.
Madeline Lanham, Grade 2
Buckner Elementary School, KY

Animals
animals
come in all shapes and sizes
animals at the pet store
animals at the shelter
ready to go explore the world

buy me! buy me! I'm so cute
fuzzy wuzzy very funny!

gerbils, squeaking cats meowing
everyone is chit chatting
come on we're going to be late!
for what?
the zoo!
lions roaring zebras screaming.
what a crazy day!
animals
come in all shapes and sizes.
Sarah Jackson, Grade 3
Camden Station Elementary School, KY

Biscuit
You always put your slobbery tongue on me
When you slept on my sheets
Circled up in a ball
You were doing your everyday thing
And I loved it

Until I moved
But you have a better home now
I love you
I hope nothing ever happens to you

Caleb Bergquist, Grade 3
Buckner Elementary School, KY

I Want a World Where...
I want a world where...
Leaves dance around like people.
Clouds are my pillow when I am tired.
I can fly in the sky like birds.
Everything is as clean as a whistle.
Whistles sing like birds.
Children can float in their rooms like astronauts.
School students are angels.
The rain kisses me on my forehead.
I want a world where...

Akiira Hill, Grade 3
Rivelon Elementary School, SC

I Want a World Where...
I want a world where...
Houses are beautiful as colorful butterflies.
Poems are everywhere like people.
The wind whistles songs in my ear.
Corn falls in my mouth like little drops of rain.
Colorful pebbles are like rainbows.
My family is the pretty color of blue.
My mom is pretty as classy shoes.
My hands are a soft furry cat.
I want a world where...

Ariyanna Williams, Grade 3
Rivelon Elementary School, SC

Elk Lake

Waking up to the early sunshine rising,
making hot cocoa, collecting strands of bacon and trotting outside,
there I sit listening to birds chirping, cricket creaking.
Quiet things.

Odors fill the air, including the smell of wet dogs and the damp
smell of lake water.
Watching fierce deer sprinting throughout the dense forest.
My heart pumping wildly.
Seeing bright white beautiful trumpeter swans skim across the water.
I'm in paradise seeing all these finely painted flower and oddly shaped clouds.
Early risers.

Sun setting, leaves fallen,
breeze cooling, daytime past away,
the crickets have grown quiet
while the lightning bugs reactivate and turn on all their lights.
Frogs croaking, water splashed all over the place,
with on last blow I find myself at the rocky shoreline
taking in deep breaths
as wind brushes harshly against my face
wondering to myself of a more beautiful place than where I am now.
Elk Lake.

Abby Maggard, Grade 3
Camden Station Elementary School, KY

A Good Book

Oh how I love a good book!
At the library it is always fun to look.
Fiction or Nonfiction I don't care,
just an adventure to take me somewhere.

Now I have found the right one,
and my search is finally done.
Back to my house I will go.
It is there my learning will grow.

Each book has its story to share.
Just open a book if you dare.
Then you still see like me,
books are great, don't you agree?

Hannah Bregman, Grade 3
Virginia A Boone Highland Oaks Elementary School, FL

I Am Grateful

I am thankful for my head
because it helps me think in class.
I am grateful for books
so I can learn to read.
I am grateful for my teeth
because I can eat macaroni,
chicken, and cheeseburgers.
Teeth are good for biting
and bobbing for apples.
I can make a tapping noise with them
and they are good for smiling.

Amir Taylor, Grade 2
Lee A Tolbert Community Academy, MO

Snaky

Snake snake
I'm a snake
I try to pickup a rake
I will try to sliver up your arm
I will not harm
I'm wide awake
'Cause I like to eat cake!
My mother calls me Brakey
My father calls me Wakey
My brother calls me Rakey
but my real name is Snaky!

Kaleb Koehn, Grade 3
Hillsdale Christian School, OK

Fall

In fall
Leaves fall off the trees.
In fall
Leaves fall on the ground.
In fall
The leaves make a bed.
In fall
The leaves scatter.
The squirrels chatter.
In fall
The weather gets cold.

Ashley Gray, Grade 2
Eagle's View Academy, FL

A Snowy Winter

The snow falling
   down
      down falling through the icy air
I freeze up like solid ice cubes.

I open the warm smooth knob
I'm in I drink burning cocoa
I'm burning melting of warmness.

Winter
Snow falling

Matthew Wedding, Grade 3
Buckner Elementary School, KY

The Beautiful Sea

The sea the sea
I think it likes me.
With buried treasure
And beautiful weather
That is where I want to be.
With waves so high
They brush the sky.
With birds so swift
They could give me a lift.
O the sea the sea
That is where I want to be.

Austin Ashbaugh, Grade 3
Columbia Catholic School, MO

The Crusty Crab

Oh, Crusty Crab
You are so beautiful
With big claws and
A spread out tail
You are so beautiful
Sitting on my plate
A bright beautiful red
You are so beautiful
Tastes good to eat you
Your shell is still there
And you are still so beautiful

Adan Aguirre, Grade 2
Kerr Elementary School, OK

Volleyball Is Fun

Volleyball is fun.
It's more fun under the sun.
It's better for everyone.
The sun is hot.
The shadow of the ball is shaped like a dot.
Don't hit the net.
The ball is what you're trying to get.
Try to jump.
The bad part is it will make a huge thump.
That might cause a bump.
It should be sunny.
Don't act funny.
Try to hit the ball in the air.
Do it! I don't care, just don't stare.
Don't hit the pole.
That might cause a hole.
Never lose control!

Varun Kasibhatla, Grade 2
Creek View Elementary School, GA

Every Day

Every day I go to play.
Then, I have to say
"Dad, I know the way."
When I go to the park…
It's not a surprise when I hear the same dog bark.
It's not too long
until the birds start to sing a song.
That's my way of spending the day.

Ben Games, Grade 3
Central Elementary School, WV

Thanksgiving Day

Thanksgiving Day is lots of fun.
It takes a while till it is done.
On Thanksgiving Day we have a feast,
With ham, turkey, and lots of meat.
When the feast is done, we visit and talk,
And when you get bored, you go on a walk.
At the end of the day, we go out and play,
With all of our friends on this cool sunny day.

Sari Jackson, Grade 3
Many Elementary School, LA

Summer

So hot I'm going to die!
That's the blazing heat
Of summer.

Get a glass of lemonade
The sun is so hot

In the summer
It seems like you've got zapped
By 5 million bolts of lightning.
120 degrees in Arizona.
Going fishing with Grandpa and catching bass.

Vincent Tinebra, Grade 3
Camden Station Elementary School, KY

Where I'm From

I am from McDonald's double cheeseburgers.
I am from my dad's awesome pork.
I am from my fun Nintendogs
I am from my grandma's meatballs.
I am from my uncle's juicy corn.
I am from Rally's cheeseburgers
I am from my dad's delicious steak.
I am from the awesome Beech Bend Park.
I am from the water park.
I am from twisted Twister.
I am from all the toys in Toys R Us.
I am from Yatzee game.

Trinity Schumacher, Grade 3
Alvaton Elementary School, KY

Scary Sight

A cemetery filled with ghosts
That say "boo" when you come up to them.
Mummies that are freaky,
Witches flying across the moon;
Bloody zombies going into a haunted house.
A tree that is scary in the night,
A coyote howling in the night sky,
Oh, now it's time for bed.
Let's have a good dream instead!

Bianca DeSilva, Grade 2
Wellington School, FL

Just Like Mom
Once there was a mom,
and her name was Michelle Spencer Louden,
and her whole body smells like strawberry perfume.

Her long, brown, spiky hair
that she makes every day
and it looks great
and her hair smells like
Got 2b Playful marshmallow.

Her beautiful blue eyes,
and her shiny teeth
in the bright, beautiful gleaming in the sun
and the voice of an angel coming down from Heaven
and touching you and blessing you

When you're telling me "go clean up your room
and I'll give you two golden dollars honey," said mom.
Oh, but when she gives them to me
they are freezing ice cubes from the fridge
and frozen to ice.

Nick Spencer, Grade 3
Camden Station Elementary School, KY

One Baby Band
One day I found a pretty door
Right next to our kitchen floor.
I opened it wide, bowls with holes,
cups, cans and muffin pans I found.
A metal whisk to make some sound.
Crash Bang Crash Bang!
A star, cowboy hat I wore.
I'm a one baby band.
I took my band into the fancy dining room.
There I found pink feathers hanging from the ceiling,
pink curtains and pink walls and a violet bouncy couch.
It is not so loud in there,
But when I do my fashion baby girl band it seems to get really noisy.
Crash-Bang-Crash-Bang!
It's fun making a band like this, you can make one too!

Lesley Coleman, Grade 2
Evangelical Christian School, TN

I Am From
I am from a loving family.
To my play fort.
I am from caring friends.
To chocolate.
I am from a loving dog.
To my cat.
I am from wild fires.
To beautiful flowers.
I am from reading July Blume.
To staying up all night.
I am from curling up under my blankets.
To being cold on sunny days.

I am from many things but those are my favorite.
Stephanie Scott, Grade 3
Buckner Elementary School, KY

The Scariest Roller Coaster
People flashing,
On the roller coaster
While I am waiting in line.

Rumbling inside the roller coaster,
A big hill comes up
And then a swoosh!
Coming down.
Excitement going through my head
Breeze blowing into my face
Two more hills to go
When the roller coaster passed the two hills
It stopped
That was an awesome roller coaster.
Jack Marcum, Grade 3
Buckner Elementary School, KY

The Sunny Sun
Oh how great is the sun.
It moves around the earth.
Her rays are like a scorching furnace.
How she stings when she touches your body.
The sweet little sunny shine.
Mikell Jenkins, Grade 1
Oakland Primary School, SC

Christmas Day
Today is Christmas
Yes it is now we hang up the Christmas tree
and we open the Christmas presents

Siras Keyse, Grade 1
Riverhill School, AL

Lizard
I see a lizard.
It jumps over the river.
And it is chubby.

Kensley Corneille, Grade 2
Virginia A Boone Highland Oaks Elementary School, FL

Waterfalls
Waterfalls are cool.
I like to see them at school.
Waterfalls like us.

Jennifer Schlaen, Grade 2
Virginia A Boone Highland Oaks Elementary School, FL

Iguanas
Iguanas are green.
They like moisture in the air.
Iguanas are cool.

Leo Saperstein, Grade 2
Virginia A Boone Highland Oaks Elementary School, FL

Turtles
Turtles can swim fast.
But they move very slowly.
Turtles are the best.

James Critz, Grade 2
Virginia A Boone Highland Oaks Elementary School, FL

Butterflies
I like butterflies.
I like their colors on them.
They are so pretty.

Angel Teate, Grade 2
Virginia A Boone Highland Oaks Elementary School, FL

Take a Venture to the Past

It's like it always has to last with you
I love to play in your back yard every day
Your heart is as bright
As the night

I love to play at the put-put play off
And go to the track with bumper boats
I love to race go carts
With my cousin at your house

We play all day with you like it never has to end
We always go to Crystal's to eat
We like the movies they play
At the new movie theatre

We love to play with you at the beach
Getting in the wet salty sand is so sweet
We love to go to Mellow Mushroom
And play on the mushroom head men

I love your smile it's so bright and inviting
And you always say — "No fighting."
I love you forever, MeMe
Love,
Luke

Luke Owings, Grade 3
A H Watwood Elementary School, AL

My Grandmother

My grandmother is always nice to me
She is always telling me that I'm doing great
She took me to the Dollar General to get me
A posterboard and markers for the poster contest at the Fall Festival
She is really awesome and
She always lightens
Up my heart
She always tells me that I'm doing great
Or awesome or smart
No matter where you are
Near or far
You will always be in my heart

Justin Wilson, Grade 3
A H Watwood Elementary School, AL

Christmas
The tree is up
Cookies are done
Time to go to sleep

As I'm asleep
I think about the presents
I'm going to get
Like a DSI
I hear something
Crack, crack, crack

When I wake up
I run downstairs
"Get up it's time!"

"Time to get up!"
"Why!"
"To open presents"

After we open presents
Let's go outside and play
Alicia Manning, Grade 3
Camden Station Elementary School, KY

Kentucky Football
Kentucky football kids zooming by
Grass winding out
He jukes 1 he jukes 2 he jukes 3 he's gone
Touchdown!
1 min left
Kickoff seeing the ball glide
There's the catch
Crushed!
Fumble!
Defense recovers break
15 seconds left
There's the snap
A far throw...
TOUCHDOWN!

Kentucky wins! 13-7
James Luke Leeper, Grade 2
Buckner Elementary School, KY

Love Is You
I love you
You love me
You are always there for me
I love you
Like a bird is always flying
In the sky always

I love you
Like a pumpkin pie
I love you when I see
The beautiful blue sky
Forever
I love you
When you cook me
The big, perfect, apple pie
Yummy Yummy

I love you
Like a scary scarecrow
Scaring away
All my fears
I love you for so many reasons
Forever
Jailah Swain, Grade 3
Childersburg Elementary School, AL

Wind
Blowing gently,
Howling loud.
Making curves
From the cloud.

Blowing hard now,
From the sky.
Oh, I wonder,
Wonder why?

The clouds are blowing
Far away.
It has been
A windy day!
Dylan Hester, Grade 3
Love Memorial Elementary School, NC

Ice Cream

Ice cream, ice cream
I love ice cream
I want to eat it
with my family.
I wish I could have some now,
I asked my mom
But she was outside planting,
I didn't want to mess up
her work.
When she was done,
I said, "Please, may I have some
Ice cream?"
She said, "Yes!"

KaLeyah Hilton, Grade 1
Cool Spring Elementary School, NC

Storms

Boom
Goes the thunder
Slash
Goes the lightning

There goes the power
Now it is pitch black
Plug up the generator
The fridge is working
The TV is working
The power is working

The rain starts drying up

Evan Myers, Grade 2
Buckner Elementary School, KY

I Love

I love to read.
I love to play sports.
I help my parents and I help my friends.
My parents love roses
Roses are red
Violets are blue
I love God and so should you!

Branden Rogers, Grade 1
Evangelical Christian School, TN

Ghost

If I were a ghost
I would go to a haunted house,
float in the air
and watch people dance
because they are frightened.
I would spin and vibrate
on people's shoulders,
whisper in their ear,
and tickle them so they can giggle.
I would twirl them around,
spin through the snow
and make snow angels.

LeAndrea Salary, Grade 3
Lee A Tolbert Community Academy, MO

Kangaroos

Kangaroos
bounce bounce bouncing high
bouncing by
bouncing low
bouncing fast
bouncing slow
bounce bounce bouncing
bounce bounce got away
bounce bounce getting food
bounce bounce got some food
bounce bounce now we are done
Kangaroos

Bryce Lifferth, Grade 3
Camden Station Elementary School, KY

Santa

When Santa comes
What a happy family time!
Opening presents
And eating lots of good food!

We will play in the snow
And ride four wheelers
And throw snowballs
At each other!

Scott Collie, Grade 3
Carver Elementary School, NC

Gobble Up Thanksgiving
I gobble up Thanksgiving.
Yes I really do.
I really like turkey,
Yes I really do!
I run all around the room just to hear mom say,
We are having turkey on Thanksgiving Day!

Lacie Stovall, Grade 1
Doyle Elementary School, LA

School
The summer is through.
It was the first day of school and everybody was mad.
And no one liked it because they were not in the mood.
The principal came to the office.
Mrs. Flagg said no running or screaming.
Hmmmm, said Mrs. Flagg.

Tyshawn Hinton, Grade 2
Mount Olive Elementary School, MS

Drugs Are Bad
Drugs are very very bad
and if you use drugs it's very very sad.
So, don't use drugs in any way because
it will make your lungs get black and
it will not make your life the way you want it.
I just wanted to let you know to not use drugs.

Haylei Powell, Grade 2
Mount Olive Elementary School, MS

My Dog
My dog is very muddy.
His name is Buddy.
When it is dark.
Sometimes he will bark.

Hannah Aversa, Grade 2
Virginia A Boone Highland Oaks Elementary School, FL

Daisy
The daisy so bright
Petals yellow like the sun
They smell delightful

Marissa Manley, Grade 3
Virginia A Boone Highland Oaks Elementary School, FL

I Want a World Where...

I want a world where...
Clever pencils jump up and down in notebooks.
Roses are colorful as rainbows.
Friends stick together like glue.
My smile is bright as the sun.
Mrs. Yarbrough is pretty as the color pink.
Frosted flakes swim in my bowl.
My friend Kaleigh's brain is a computer.
My favorite shirt is like the blue sky.
I want a world where...

Tiyana Dash, Grade 3
Rivelon Elementary School, SC

I Want a World Where...

I want a world where...
My dad is tall as a tree.
McDonald's says come in and eat.
Leaves can dance on my head in the fall.
Life is forever.
The grass talks as I walk on it.
The days of the week are as slow as a snail.
I am a fish in water.
Water is as shiny as a diamond.
I want a world where...

Kevin Wigfall, Grade 3
Rivelon Elementary School, SC

I Want a World Where...

I want a world where...
Happiness comes and goes to homes around the world.
Grass dances on my feet as soft as a pillow.
My friends stick together like two peas in a pod.
Rice jumps in my mouth and says eat me.
My red shoes dance on the dance floor.
My pillow is soft as a cloud.
I can fly like a bird in the blue sky.
My book whispers words in my ear.
I want a world where...

Shercara Baker, Grade 3
Rivelon Elementary School, SC

Autumn Is Everything

I can see autumn.
I can see scary looking pumpkins.
I can see the darkest sky in the world.
I can see funny and scary costumes.

I can smell autumn.
I can smell fresh pumpkins.
I can smell good tasting candy.
I can smell freshly baked pumpkin pie.

I can hear autumn.
I can hear my dog howling at the moon.
I can hear people knocking on doors saying Happy Halloween.
I can hear spooky owls going hoo hoo.

I can taste autumn.
I can taste the best ham in the world.
I can taste juicy cider.
I can taste very healthy stuffing.

I don't need to look at the calendar to know that it's autumn.

Sage Bayruns, Grade 3
The Parke House Academy, FL

Adam Reed Singer

A thletic
D etermined
A wesome
M ajestic

R espectful
E asy
E ight
D elightful

S ilent
I ntelligent
N ice
G reedy
E nergetic
R ebellious

Adam Reed Singer, Grade 3
Virginia A Boone Highland Oaks Elementary School, FL

The Rose
Glittering rose
In the morning sunlight
As white as snow can be

Three leaves
On each side
This little flower
Is such a sight

A little thin stem
Bright green
White petals
That beautiful rose

So lonely and quiet
No friends
Not even a little flower
Nearby
So lonely
So cold

Speaking to itself
"It's all right, it's all right."
This little flower
Olivia Curell, Grade 3
Buckner Elementary School, KY

Winter Night
Snow floating through the air
Washing down and down
On the ground,
Of the icy snow blistering
Around my face,
Floating in the breeze
Putting it in my mouth
Like an ice cream.
My tongue is frozen
From the silky snow,
The frigid
Winter
Night.
Alexis Head, Grade 3
Buckner Elementary School, KY

Fall Leaf
I want to be a leaf
and I can blow away,
fall off trees,
or feel warm or cold.
Water falls on me.
I can take baths in the rain
and look red and yellow.
I hear people stepping on me.
Mostly, I can watch cart wheels.
When the wind blows,
we huddle around each other.
We sing or pray when we fall.
Shanique Carmons, Grade 3
Lee A Tolbert Community Academy, MO

If I Were a Squirrel
If I were a squirrel
I would climb trees and
Eat nuts all day
I would hide in trees
If I were a squirrel
I would run in the water
And fly through the sky
If I were a squirrel
I would camp all day and night
If I were a squirrel
I would fall in a pile of leaves
If I were a squirrel
Kyler Pritchard, Grade 2
Buckner Elementary School, KY

Star and Moon
Look at the little star
Shining bright.
It outshines the moon
Way up in the sky so high!

You can fall asleep
Watching them there
Up in the sky
So high!
Tajjaquan Person, Grade 3
Carver Elementary School, NC

New Born Katie

Small as a mouse
Her cute pink outfit
Covers her small little body
Head to toe in a clear crib
Small little brown eyes like a garden full of dirt
Little tiny toes on a blanket.
New Born Katie

As she opens her eyes
I wonder if she's ready for the day
To play in her play pen
She makes a grin on her face.
New Born Katie

Her mom comes in
And puts her in her high chair
To eat breakfast.
New Born Katie

She eats and eats
Till her tummy is full
Her mom pats her on the back
Pat…Pat…Pat until she burps…
Buurrrp. New Born Katie

Monica Olvera, Grade 3
Camden Station Elementary School, KY

Where I'm From

I am from Pizza Hut's hot pizza right out of the stove.
I am from steak well done off of the grills.
I am from Ritz crackers from an antique can.
I am from french fries super salty.
I am from Junior Monopoly beating my sister.
I am from card games Triple Solitaire.
I am from night tag my mom's cousin made up.
I am from playing my video games like Pokémon.
I am from frog hunting at my dad's pond.
I am from hunting for deer at my paw place.
I am from Brock who I have known 3 years.
I am from Jackson who has been a great friend to me for 4 years.
I am from Cannan who has been in my class for 4 years.

Cruz McClure, Grade 3
Alvaton Elementary School, KY

I Like to Box

I box a fox.
Every day I box a fox in boxing gloves.
The fox boxed me.
I was boxing him too.
Me and him boxed all the time.
I box a fox in boxing gloves.

Tyler Strout, Grade 3
Alpena Elementary School, AR

Brown and Yellow Leaves

Leaves fall on the ground,
it's fall again.
I put leaves in a pile and
I jump and play in the
brown and yellow leaves.
I have lots of fun in the fall.

Jacari Mixon, Grade 1
Oakland Primary School, SC

Mom

I love my mom.
She smells good and is the best.
I love how she cooks
and when I look in her eyes
they are pretty
and so is her heart.

Marqeies Johnson, Grade 2
Lee A Tolbert Community Academy, MO

The Christmas Bear

There once a bear,
he loved to share.
He gave me a toy,
it brought me great joy.
I call him the Christmas Bear
because he loved to share!

Emily Garner James, Grade 2
Macon-East Montgomery Academy, AL

All About Trees

Some trees have green leaves.
Some leaves are orange.
Some leaves are red.
Some leaves are yellow.
Some leaves are brown.
Some trees don't have leaves.

Gavyn Mathes, Grade 1
Oakland Primary School, SC

Santa

Santa is here with a lot of toys
he gives them to girls and boys.
Santa is fun and fat,
he always sits on a mat.
Santa comes once a year,
with all of his reindeer.

Tyson Tubbs, Grade 2
Macon-East Montgomery Academy, AL

I See a Bee

Buzz, buzz
I see a bee
buzz, buzz
it's near that tree
buzz, buzz
don't sting me!

Alex Wodicka, Grade 1
Oakland Primary School, SC

Christmas Day

On Christmas Day
I got to sit on a sleigh.
Santa gave me a gift,
a toy crane with a lift.
It is cool as can be,
and it is special to me!

Judson Waters, Grade 2
Macon-East Montgomery Academy, AL

Volleyball
We play our exciting game of volleyball
Seeing the team on the other side.
Who is gonna win the exciting game?
Hope we win the exciting game.
We smack it
Yah come on. Get it!
Then my turn to serve
Feeling the nerves.
Will someone go before me?
I think in my mind.
The volleyball as squishy as foam.
In my hand READY! I've got to do this I think. I can now.
Here I go…Boom Boom ball on ground.
OUT! Hhhhh.
Two more turns.
Hit OUT! Hhhh
Here I go again
YES!
I did it
One Awesome Game!
WE WIN!

Audrey Gast, Grade 2
Buckner Elementary School, KY

Imagine a World…
Imagine a world…
with lots of things to do
like going to the lake
and looking at your reflection.

Imagine a world…
with sweets and flowers and candy
and adventure and experiences.

Imagine a world…
with stars and love and color and art
but most of all with care.

Imagine a world.

Ellynn Nickens-Hill, Grade 3
Robert E Lee Expressive Arts Elementary School, MO

Shimmer River
Calm ripples
Tickling me

To you
It may be a river

To me
It's a glorious sight

Like
A never before
Seen river

Like
A secret message
Telling me it's like glass
As fragile as can be
Like a mirror
With clouds
Like cotton candy
Parker Chace, Grade 3
Buckner Elementary School, KY

The Sea
Sea snakes
Slithering
Around you
Stingray
Stinging
Its prey
Sharks
Wagging
Their
Tail fin
Like
A rag
Dolphin
Singing
Eeeee
Jumping out
Like a whale
Ricky Green, Grade 2
Buckner Elementary School, KY

Itchie
Barks
Licks me
Wags his tail
Bites the UPS man
Loves me.
David Austin Wood, Grade 1
Oakland Primary School, SC

Basketball
Basketball, basketball.
I like to play.
Basketball, basketball all day.
Ran fast, ran slow
See how I go
Jamison Holmes, Grade 1
Oakland Primary School, SC

My Mom
My mom takes real good care of me.
Even though she is sick
she helps me with my homework.
She cooks for me, plays with me.
Also we cook together, and pray together.
Aliyah China, Grade 1
Oakland Primary School, SC

My Dog Ebony
My dog Ebony loves me.
My dog Ebony likes to go to the river.
My dog Ebony likes to play with her ball.
She likes to go to the park.
My dog Ebony likes to sleep.
Demitrî Beasley, Grade 1
Oakland Primary School, SC

Little Hamster
I bring my hamster home from Petco.
I keep him in a cage.
Little is his first name.
Hamster is his last name.
He likes his bed.
Spencer Smith, Grade 1
Oakland Primary School, SC

Butterfly
Fly butterfly fly to the sky.
See the other butterflies.
Then fly home.
Anthony Cole Lewis, Grade 1
Oakland Primary School, SC

Cat
C is for cute.
A is for angry.
T is for Tiger.
Levi Hartley, Grade 1
New York Elementary School, MO

Index

Author Autograph Page

Author Autograph Page

Author Autograph Page

Author Autograph Page

Author Autograph Page

Author Autograph Page